HOME BREWED BEERS AND STOUTS

by
C. J. J. BERRY

Editor, "The Amateur Winemaker and Home Brewer"

A HANDBOOK TO THE BREWING OF ALES, BEERS AND STOUTS AT HOME FROM BARLEY, MALT, MALT EXTRACT AND DRIED MALT EXTRACT

"THE AMATEUR WINEMAKER"

Publications, Dormer House, South Street
Andover, Hampshire

Printed in Great Britain by
Standard Press (Andover) Ltd., Wolfe Street, Andover, Hants.
Tel. 2413

© THE AMATEUR WINEMAKER

FIRST EDITION	1963
SECOND EDITION	1966
THIRD EDITION	1970
FOURTH EDITION	1970
NINETEENTH IMPRESSION	1979
TWENTIETH IMPRESSION	1980
TWENTY-FIRST IMPRESSION	1981
TWENTY-SECOND IMPRESSION	1981

SBN 900841 02 8

Published by the Amateur Winemaker
Andover, Hampshire

Printed in Great Britain by:
Standard Press (Andover) Ltd., South Street, Andover, Hants
Tel. 2413

CONTENTS

"*The process of brewing ought to form a part of the domestic economy of every family . . . the greater part of the population of this great and free country are doomed to destroy their health by the consumption of the intoxicating stupefactive compositions of the porter quacks and beer doctors, which are daily passing into their stomachs in the form of pothouse slops or wash, under misnomers of porter, ale, intermediate beer or that nondescript and indefinable compound, London small or table beer.*"

—William Cobbett.

About this book

BUDGET DAY, April 3rd, 1963, was a memorable day for the thousands of home brewers in this country.

On that day Mr. Reginald Maudling, then Chancellor of the Exchequer, abolished Excise restrictions upon brewing beer at home; no longer was it necessary to have a private brewer's licence or to pay duty upon the beer you produced. You are free to brew as much beer as you like, and the only legal stipulation that must be observed is that not a drop of it must be sold. At one stroke of the pen Mr. Maudling very sensibly thus gave home brewers the same freedom in the practice of their craft as had always been enjoyed by home winemakers.

There has consequently been an upsurge in interest in brewing one's own beer, and sensible, practical instructions in the art are in some demand.

Although there are many books now on the market dealing exhaustively with winemaking, this was the first full-length book to cover in detail the home brewing of beers and stouts. It has been welcomed by the thousands who wanted to brew their own wholesome beer but who were at a loss as to how to set about it, and many thousands of the early editions have been sold. This revised and improved edition of *Home Brewed Beers and Stouts* gives you not only the background and theory of brewing but instructions and recipes for ales, beers and stouts of all types, from the lightest lager to a black stout, and with its aid you will turn out brews of which you can be really proud. It tells how to utilise barley, malt and malt extract (liquid or dried), and how to make "mock" beers as well.

American readers should note that 1 Imperial, or English, gallon equals 1.2 U.S. gallons, and adapt the recipes accordingly.

5

For convenience, where a recipe says 1, 2, 3, 4 or 5 gallons they should substitute respectively 1½, 2½, 3½, 5 and 6 gallons.

Although the basic principles of brewing are the same as those of winemaking in that both are a process of fermentation, the technique, it will be seen, is rather different, if the best results are to be obtained. In some respects it is more tricky to brew a quality beer than it is to make a quality wine, but it is therefore more intriguing. And the home brewer has the advantage over the winemaker that his product is ready for consumption within a month or so.

Beer, our national drink, is not only thirst-quenching and enjoyable; it is also nourishing. It is a fact that a pint of strong beer has the same food value as a pint of milk (about 400 calories). Beer is rich in several B complex vitamins and home-brewed beer, especially, is a healthy, unadulterated drink. One often hears the comment that "There's nothing like bread and cheese and a glass of beer," and, strangely enough, it could well be claimed that chemically and nutritionally this is indeed the perfect meal.

Do not be misled by anyone "in the trade" who has a vested interest in commercial beer sales, or by anyone else who tells you that it is not possible to brew an excellent beer using the simplest apparatus, or that home brew is of inferior quality. It is perfectly possible to brew a beer every bit as high in quality as that which can be obtained in your "local", and the more you study the subject the more you will realise why: you are using exactly the same ingredients as the commercial brewer, and similar methods, albeit on a smaller scale; and there is no reason at all why you should NOT succeed, and succeed dramatically. After all, at one time every public house and inn—and many a home—brewed its own beer, and commercial brewing on a massive, "amalgamated" scale is but the product of modern times.

There is great satisfaction in being able to offer a friend a tankard of your own good ale. The economy of home brewing is dramatic, too; its basic cost can be as little as 6p a pint!

Home brewing is a fascinating and rewarding pastime, undertaken intelligently, and this is the book to set you on the right track. Good brewing!

C. J. J. BERRY

Brewing Vocabulary

ACETIC ACID:

The acid formed when beer is left exposed to the air and turns vinegary.

ACROSPIRE:

Shoot which grows from grain of barley during malting.

ALE:

Formerly, unhopped beer.

ATTENUATION:

The drop in a wort's specific gravity as sugar is used up during fermentation.

BARLEY:

Grain most commonly used for brewing.

BARLEY WINE:

A very strong beer. See page 21.

BARM:

Mixture of wort and yeast.

BEER:

Hopped ale.

BEST BITTER:

A high-quality pale ale. See page 21.

BOTTOMS:

Deposits of yeasts and solids formed during fermentation.

BREWERS' GRAINS:

The insoluble residue of malt left in mash tun after the wort has been run off.

BREWERS' YEAST:

A top-fermenting strain of *Saccharomyces cerevisiae*. This yeast ferments on the surface of the wort, forming floating islands of yeast, which subsequently sink. Lager yeast (*S. Carlsbergensis*) is bottom fermenting.

BROWN ALE:

A medium-strength, darker beer. See page 21.

BURNT SUGAR:

Old name for caramel colouring: prepared from glucose.

BURTON WATER:

A description applied to water of similar hardness to that found at Burton-onTrent, important in the brewing of pale ales.

BUSH:

Ancient sign for an inn (hence: "Good wine needs no bush.") Probably of Roman origin; a "bush" of ivy and vine leaves was the symbol of the wine-god, Bacchus.

BUSH:

Metal liner of the bung or tap-hole of a barrel.

CALCIUM SULPHATE:

One of the chemicals which gives water a permanent hardness. Popularly called gypsum or Plaster of Paris.

CARBON DIOXIDE:

Gas given off during fermentation which gives the "head" on beer, and the sparkle.

CARAMEL:

See BURNT SUGAR.

CASKS:

Butt, 108 gallons; Puncheon, 72 gallons; Hogshead, 54 gallons; Barrel, 36 gallons; Kilderkin, 18 gallons; Firkin, 9 gallons; Pin, 4¼ gallons.

CONDITION:

The "life" a beer has owing to the carbon dioxide in it

CYTASE:

Enzyme in barley grain which dissolves the cellulose protecting the granule and allows fermentation to proceed.

DEXTRINS:

Substances in wort released during mashing.

DIASTASE:

Enzyme in barley which converts starch to fermentable sugar.

DRAUGHT:

Beer served from the barrel.

ENZYMES:

Catalysts in the barley grain which affect malting during the mashing process.
See CYTASE, DIASTASE, INVERTASE, MALTASE, and ZYMASE.

FERMENTATION:

Yeast working upon a sugar solution (the wort) to produce alcohol and carbon dioxide.

FERMENTATION LOCK:

A little gadget to protect the brew from bacterial contamination.

FININGS:

Used for removing suspended solids from cloudy beer: usually isinglass or Irish Moss.

FLAKES:

Maize, rice or barley can be used as an adjunct to malt during mashing; it has already been "pre-cooked".

FOBBING:

Overlively beer foaming up out of the bottle. Usually the beer has been kept in too warm a place or has been overprimed, or the bottle has been overfilled.

GALLON:

8 pints, 160 liq. oz., or 277¼ cu. inches (American gallon, 128 oz.). 1 Imperial or English Gallon = 1.2 U.S. gallon.
Equivalents:

English	1	2	3	4	5 gallons
American	1¼	2½	3½	4½	6 gallons

GILL:

Usually ¼ pint, but in some areas ½ pint (of ale).

GLUCOSE:

A directly fermentable sugar purchased in the form of "glucose chippings", large lumps, light brown in colour. Ferments well and imparts a little colour.

GOODS:

See **GRIST.**

GRAVITY.

The density or weight of a liquid.

GREEN MALT:

Germinated barley before it is kilned.

GRIST:

The blended grain used in malting barley after it has been malted and crushed. Also called "Goods".

GRIT:

Any grain, other than barley, used in brewing. Raw and not prepared, like flakes.

GYPSUM:

Calcium sulphate or plaster of Paris. An important constituent of water ("or liquor") if beer is to clear well.

HARDNESS:

Quality in water desirable when brewing bitters or lights. *See* **CALCIUM SULPHATE.**

HEAD:

The froth on beer. Good head retention is important, and is found in a well-conditioned beer with a good malt content, adequately hopped, since these factors contribute to its having sufficient surface tension.

HEADING LIQUID:

Used for adding an artificial "head".

HOP:

The flower of the hop plant (*humulus lupulus*) used in beer for its preservative and flavouring qualities

HOP OIL:

A concentrate which can be used instead of dry hopping. It needs to be handled with care, for 1 drop is enough for up to 10 gallons. Hop oil gives the beer an added zest.

10

HYDROMETER:
Instrument for measuring the sugar content of a wort and strength of finished beer.

HYDROMETER JAR:
Jar in which hydrometer is floated for a reading to be taken.

INDIA PALE ALE:
See page 21.

INVERT SUGAR:
Sugar which has been "inverted" by hydrolysis in the presence of acid. Often used in final stages of brewing, or for priming, since it ferments well.

INVERTASE:
An enzyme which breaks down sucrose into glucose and fructose, thus "inverting" it and making it fermentable.

IRISH MOSS:
A mixture of two marine algae, *chondrus crispus* and *Gigartina mamillosa*, used as a clarifying agent. It functions as a coagulant for complex and unstable proteins.

KILN:
Used in malting for drying malt after its germination.

KRAUSENING:
Adding some vigorously fermenting wort to another wort which has almost fermented out; a way of priming beer.

LACTOSE:
Milk sugar once used in Milk Stout. See page 37.

LAGER:
See page 22.

LEES:
See BOTTOMS.

LIGHT ALE:
See page 21.

LIQUOR:
In brewing—water!

11

LONDON WATER:
Soft water, as found in London, and suitable for brown ales and stouts.

LUPULIN:
Yellow powder in the hop flower containing the oils and resins which give the hop its bitterness.

MALT:
Barley which has been so treated as to convert its starch into fermentable sugar.

MALT EXTRACT:
Malt wort concentrated into a syrup of honey-like consistency—a Godsend to the modern home brewer!

MALTOSE:
The fermentable sugar obtained by malting.

MASH:
Mixture of malt and hot water, or the combination of ingredients from which the beer will be made.

MASH TUB (or TUN):
Container for mash.

MILK STOUT:
Former name for a stout in which lactose (milk sugar) has been utilised.

NOGGIN:
Quarter-pint.

NUTRIENT:
Nitrogenous matter added to wort to boost the action of the yeast; yeast food.

PALE ALE:
See page 21.

PINT:
Imperial pint—20 liq. oz.; reputed pint—a 12 oz. bottle.

PITCH:
Add yeast to the wort to cause fermentation.

POLISHING:
Filtering beer through asbestos to give it brilliance.

PORTER:
See page 22.

PRIMING:
Adding a small quantity of sugar to a jar or bottle of beer to cause a slight further fermentation and give it a head and sparkle.

QUART:
    A quarter-gallon.
QUARTER:
    336 lb. grain malt.
QUARTERN:
    A quarter-pint.
RACK:
    Siphon beer off the lees into fresh container: filling a cask
ROUSE:
    To stir or mix thoroughly, from bottom to top.
SHIVE:
    Circular wooden plug, bored centrally, used to seal a
    filled barrel.

SPARGING:
    Spraying the floating grains with hot water during
    mashing, whilst the wort is drawn off from below.
SPECIFIC GRAVITY:
    The density or weight of a liquid compared specifically
    to that of water.

SPILE:
    Small wooden peg which is a close fit in the hole in the
    shive and is loosened to admit air and allow beer to be
    drawn from the barrel. Afterwards it must be pressed
    home again or the beer will lose condition.
STILLION:
    Wooden cradle or stand for barrel.
STOUT:
    See page 22.
TORRIFIED:
    Roasted, as applied to malt.
TUN:
    Name given to many vessels in a brewery (cf. Mash Tun).
    Once a measure (wine): 252 gallons.
WORT:
    The liquid extract ready to be fermented.
YEAST:
    The fermenting agent, in brewing usually a strain of
    saccharomyces cerevisiae.
ZYMASE:
    The enzymes responsible for fermentation.

13

The Story of Ale and Beer

WHAT *is* ale or beer, and is there any difference?

It is perhaps only in this century that the two words "ale" and "beer" have come to mean almost the same. A more logical division of malt beverages today would be into "Beers" and "Stouts", hence the title of this book.

In this country today "ale" and "beer" are virtually synonymous; both denote a hopped, alcoholic drink made from malted barley, but this was not always so. Originally ale was malt liquor WITHOUT hops, and the term "beer ' was not in general use in the modern sense until hops were introduced in the fifteenth century. Beer, or "beor", it is true, is mentioned in Anglo-Saxon writings, but it is not clear whether this was malt beer or a weak form of mead. And from A.D. 950 onwards the word beor seems to drop from the language, only to reappear as "bere or "biere" in the fifteenth century (see page 18).

ALE

"Ale" is used differently in various districts and can denote almost any malt liquor except stout and porter.

The term "ale was often associated with special brewing occasions, or festivals of Old England. Thus, for university occasions, we have **Audit Ale,** originally brewed at Trinity College, Cambridge, for audit day, and subsequently by other Oxford and Cambridge colleges, **Brasenose Ale,** and **College Ale.** There were many special ales connected with rural life: **Lamb-ale,** for lambing time, **Cuckoo-ale,** for the day the cuckoo was first heard, **Leet-ale,** drunk in connection with the sitting of the old-time Courts Baron and Leet, **Harvest ale** for the ingathering of the crops, **October Ale,** and **Winter**

Ale, aided and abetted by **Mulled Ale,** for a freezing night. All in all, our forebears seem to have catered for most of the seasons! The list does not end here, for the Church contributed with **Church-ale,** for parish events, **Clerks-ale** for Easter, **Whitsun Ale,** and **Bride-ale,** the proceeds from the sale of which went to the bride. Similarly, there was **Bid-ale,** drunk at a party to which each guest brought a gift, and the reverse, **Give Ale,** a "free issue" bought as the result of a windfall or legacy.

Ale and beer, it is true to say, have been brewed in one form or another for thousands of years, not only from malted barley but from maize and millet (in Africa) and rice (in Asia). Other grain has been and still is used either in place of barley or in addition to it.

Brewing is a craft which has its origins right back in the mists of antiquity. As long ago as 4000 B.C. beer was brewed in ancient Mesopotamia, where bread was mashed, malted and fermented, and the resultant brew flavoured with spices, dates or honey.

A thousand years or so later, legend has it, Isis, the mother of the gods, introduced it to the Egypt of the Pharaohs, where at least six types of beer are thought to have been in daily use. It was known as *Boozah* or *Hequp* and became the popular national beverage. It was probably a "bitter", since it is believed to have been flavoured with rue, and cuneiform inscriptions giving detailed brewing instructions and quantities have been discovered by archaeologists. It is a whimsical thought that, 3,000 years before Christ, some now-forgotten Egyptian scribe set out to tackle exactly the same task as I do today.

It was probably from ancient Egypt that barley was first brought to Britain, so perhaps the word "booze" came with it!

The Greeks certainly "had a word for it"—*Zythos*—and the Romans called beer *cerevisia*. In parts of France even today the old name for beer—*cervoise*—is still used instead of the modern *bière*, which derives from the German. *Cerevisia* stood originally for a weak mead, or honey beer, and the word is seen again in the Latin name for brewer's yeast—*saccharomyces cerevisiae*. The Romans had beer as well as wine as an everyday drink, and rated it highly; Lucullus, the classic epicure, served it in golden goblets at his banquets and Julius Caesar gave it to his successful commanders.

Fermented drinks of one sort or another were being brewed in Britain before recorded history began, but they were probably meads made from the honey of wild bees, and it is not clear whether any malt liquors were made before the Roman invasion, but certainly during the 400 years of the Roman occupation ale was consumed in quantity in these islands, for in the Legions would be many recruited from elsewhere in Europe to whom beer was, like wine to others, one of the essentials of life. The Romans may thus have introduced the British to ale and the hop. Certainly the Britons, the Picts and the Scots all knew how to brew, and ale was served at their feasts and important celebrations.

When the Romans left, and the Saxons and Vikings descended upon Britain, brewing was one craft which persisted, for the Northmen were lovers of ale, quaffing it from drinking horns before battle and in their redoubtable feastings.

Ale houses became numerous, so much so that "Edgar the Peaceable", King of Wessex, had many of them closed, ordaining that there should be not more than one per village. At this period, too, drinking mugs were marked with pegs to define the size of a swig, and facilitate drinking contests! Hence our phrase about "taking someone down a peg . . ."

The Normans, too, were no strangers to malt liquor, and in the settled centuries after the Conquest brewing for the first time became feasible on a really large scale. Mostly it was the province of the monasteries and church, and the Domesday Book, for instance, records that the monks of St. Paul's Cathedral brewed 67,814 gallons of ale from 175 quarters each of wheat and barley and 708 quarters of oats. One cannot be exact because of variations in measures, but that would be probably three times as strong as modern beers! Knowledge of brewing was as widespread as that of tea-making today, and every housewife could turn her hand to it.

16

The first tax on ale (Henry II's impost on "movables") was levied in 1188 and from then on there were various enactments to control both quality and price, such as Henry III's Assize of Bread and Ale (1267) which tied the price of these commodities to those of grain and malt, and which lasted for three centuries. Heavy penalties were imposed upon bakers or brewers whose products did not come up to the mark in quantity or quality, so in the fourteenth century we find that well-known official, the ale-conner, or ale-taster, being introduced.

At this time there was, of course, no mechanical way of assessing a brew's worth so the ale-taster had authority to taste any brewer's ale, and order its price to be lowered if it was not satisfactory. The ale-conner (or al-konnere) wore leather breeches, and the practical test he employed was to pour some beer on a barrel end, and sit on it for a specified period. If, when he rose, his breeches stuck momentarily to the barrel, the beer was up to standard!

My own borough of Andover until 1973 had an official ale-taster who was solemnly appointed at Mayor-making each year but he no longer took the oath of office and certainly did not wear leather breeches . . .

The Middle Ages were a great period of expansion and improvement in brewing. Ale was the national beverage, and honey the common sweetener, since sugar did not become popularly available until the middle of the eighteenth century. At first each ale house brewed its own, but gradually breweries sprang up, each supplying several houses, and in time these grew in size and importance. Much of the brewing was in the hands of the church, which sold ale to raise money for special purposes, so that the word "ale" came also to be used to denote a special function or occasion for fund-raising purposes.

Brewing had become an accepted craft, and was given standing by Royal decree in 1406 when the Worshipful Company of Brewers—which still exists—was recognised as "the Mistery of Free Brewers"; in 1437 it was granted a charter by Henry VI to exercise control over "the brewing of any kind of malt liquor in the City and its suburbs for ever".

BEER

It was in the fourteenth century, too, that hops were introduced and the word "beer" reappeared. Hitherto Britain had drunk the fermented malt drink called "ale", but soldiers returning from the Hundred Years War (1338–1453) missed and demanded the drink to which they had become accustomed in northern France and Flanders, *"bere"* or *"bière"*. This was an ale flavoured with hops, which then grew only on the Continent and not in Britain (where they were not planted before 1525). The Romans may have used them, but after their departure ale was flavoured in many ways with other herbs—nettles, rosemary, alecost (costmary) gruit (a mixture or herbs) or even ground ivy.

Like all innovations, the hop was bitterly opposed by the traditionalists, and there was fierce competition between ale-brewers and beer-brewers, the former bringing all possible pressures to bear against the use of the "wicked, pernicious weed." They managed to have legislation passed that only water, malt, and yeast could be used in the production of ale and it was not until 1493 that beer brewers were given craft recognition as a guild.

There were no indigenous hops in England, and the Kentish hop-fields were started in 1524–5 by immigrants from the Lowlands which led to the suggestion in Sir Richard Baker's *Chronicles of the Kings of England* concerning 1524:

> *Tyrkeys, Carps, Hops, Piccarel and Beer,*
> *Came to England in one year.*

Once the hop *was* introduced (originally as a preservative), it grew more and more popular until it became eventually an essential part of the accepted flavour of beer. This process, however, took two or three centuries, and the old flavours persisted side by side with it. It is, as I have said, perhaps only in this century that "ale" and "beer" have finally come to mean the same.

The first Licensing Laws seem to have been introduced by Henry VII in 1495, and in 1552 Edward VI passed measures to control "taverns and tippling houses".

The Tudors—including Henry VIII—and the "first" Elizabethans—including Good Queen Bess—were all great beer drinkers (in those days one had beer for breakfast) and

18

beer has, despite all its rivals, really remained the national favourite ever since. The seventeenth century saw the introduction of fortified wines such as sherry and port, and of brandy, and since these were favoured by the "upper crust", beer tended to be less drunk at formal or official functions, though it remained the everyday drink of the nation.

It was a Stuart, Charles I, who imposed the first really effective taxation on beer in 1643, a trend that was continued by Charles II and his successors until nearly half the national income was derived from this source.

This went hand in hand with the development of brewing, which accelerated greatly in the eighteenth century. The middle of the century saw many still-famous breweries founded —Barclay, Bass, Charringtons, Coombe, Courage, Guinness, Meux, Simonds, Watney, Whitbread and Worthington, for instance—and brewing became truly big business, with a really impressive export trade.

This, of course, attracted yet more taxation on beer, malt and hops, and this in turn drove the people to drink cheap spirits, in England gin, in Scotland whisky; this was the dissolute period savagely lampooned by Hogarth in "Gin Row" and "The Rake's Progress".

In an effort to better conditions—and to improve the Government's popularity, then at low ebb—in 1830 taxes on beer were abolished, though those on malt and hops were retained. Licensing Laws were introduced in 1839, and have been constantly amended ever since. They still add some droll inconsistencies to the English way of life! The use of sugar in brewing was legalised in 1847.

The tax on hops was dropped in 1862 and the impact of science on the growing brewing industry made it possible for Mr. Gladstone in 1880 to abandon the tax on malt and introduce beer taxation based on specific gravity and the use of the hydrometer (or saccharometer).

At this time beers were strong, with gravities such as: strong ales 83–116; "Russian Stout" 116–131; porter 69–83; pale ale 55–69.

It was Mr. Gladstone's 1880 Act, incidentally, which applied to the home brewer, "the private brewer not for sale", a status which was determined by the rateable value of one's premises. Since this rateable value eventually became out of date and was not amended, the Act became meaningless, but it remained on the Statute Book, producing an incredibly complicated and unsatisfactory situation for would-be home brewers, right up until 1963, when Mr. Maudling removed all restrictions on home brewing.

This century, of course, has seen the disappearance of hundreds of small breweries, and the emergence of mammoth brewery combines. This has meant the disappearance, therefore, of many once-popular and highly individual brews and a gradual flattening-out of variations in beers until only a few main types now survive. Draught beer once was king, and its condition depended largely on the cellar work of the landlord, but today huge breweries bring science to their aid and more and more beer is artificially conditioned and the trend is steadily towards more and more "keg" beers. Bottled beers, too, introduced just before World War 1, have grown steadily in popularity.

Types of Beer and Stout

Whilst we cannot (and would not wish to) exactly imitate commercial beers, any more than we can copy true wines, it is obviously useful to know the principal types which are popular today, since they are the ones that appeal to the modern palate.

Ordinary ale or beer may be anywhere between 3% and 6% alcohol by volume, so that its average original gravity will have been about 30.

Other beers may be stronger, and therefore more expensive, since more malt will be used in their production and they may need longer storage.

Best Bitter: A general term for what is perhaps the highest expression of the brewer's craft, embracing Light Ale, Pale Ale, Indian Pale Ale and others of similar type, varying according to strength and hopping. All are straw-coloured, dry, and with good bite, and are popular as bottled beers. Only the lightest and finest barleys, giving a pale malt, are used, and the relatively large amount of hops used gives a pronounced hop flavour, whence this beer, as draught, gets its description as "Bitter".

Light Ale: As its name implies, this is light in both colour and texture. Smooth, dry and well hopped, with a good "bite". Should be brilliant and have good head retention. Original gravity: About 30.

Pale Ale: Slightly more "body" than light ale, slightly more strength (O.G. anywhere between 40 and 45). Slightly more hops and slightly more colour (straw to light amber). India Pale Ale was originally specially brewed in the nineteenth century to be sent to our troops in India at the time of the British Raj; Burton Ale (no longer necessarily brewed in Burton-on-Trent) has an O.G. of 45, bottled pale ales one of about 33. Pale ale should be high in malt bouquet, and well hopped, with a dry, fresh, clean taste.

Mild Ale: Varies enormously according to locality, but is usually less strong than bitter, darker in colour, less bitter (less hops) and slightly sweeter. Can be almost dark brown in colour. O.G. about 1030, alcohol 3–3½%. Once called **Four-Ale** (hence "Four-Ale Bar").

Brown Ale: Can be similar to mild, but is usually slightly heavier and stronger (e.g. Newcastle Brown, Stock Ale, and Scotch Ale). Made from darker malts, kilned at higher temperatures and perhaps roasted. O.G. 40.

Old Ale: Not quite so heavy or dark as most brown ales, but of high alcohol content and well matured. O.G. 45.

Barley Wine: Very high in alcohol (O.G. about 80, that of a dry wine); colour preferably deep garnet; full, fruity bouquet, and an almost vinous flavour. Long maturation is necessary.

21

Stout: A peculiarly British drink, not brewed on the Continent. **Dry type:** As drunk in Ireland has about 5% alcohol, derived from an O.G. of about 45. It is very dark, almost black, and is made from much-roasted (or "torrified") barley, and the head is full and creamy. The bouquet is full and the taste sharply "woody" or bitter, as the result of high hopping and the use of roasted malts. **Sweet type:** Similar, but sweetened with caramel or lactose. **Milk Stout** is *not* made partly from milk, and the name has now been abandoned. It was so called because lactose, the type of sugar found in milk, is used in its manufacture. The blackest, strongest, and most popular "Extra Stout" is made from the most heavily roasted malts and is extremely difficult to imitate.

Porter was first made in 1722 (it was then known as "Entire") and became popular in the eighteenth and nineteenth centuries, and is so still in Ireland. It was a mixture of ale, beer, and "two-penny", a pale "small" beer. In appearance it is halfway between ale and stout and, as far as can be discovered, derives its name from the fact that it was the favourite tipple of market porters in London. (Porterhouse steaks were sold at the porter-house, the tavern where porter was sold.) It is made with soft water and the original S.G. nowadays is about 40.

Lager, surprisingly enough, is quite difficult to make successfully, for it is not just a light, weak beer, as so many think, but the product of a rather different brewing system. British beers are produced by infusion and top fermentation, whereas Lager, the popular drink on the Continent and in America, is produced by decoction and bottom fermentation, with a slow secondary fermentation at a low temperature during the several months for which it is stored. In other words, it is a beer produced by a winemaking fermentation technique. The yeast employed is a special one, Saccharomyces Carlsbergensis, now available to the home brewer, and the hops are likewise usually special ones—Hallertauer or Saaz. The hopping rate is only about half that of beer. Colour should be straw (though there are *some* dark lagers to be found in Bavaria) and the lager should be lively, with good head retention. O.G.: about 1060. Taste: light, smooth, and clean, with plenty of malt and not too much hops.

Background to Brewing

THE DIFFERENCE BETWEEN BREWING AND WINE-MAKING

Both winemaking and brewing, of course, are basically a process of producing an alcoholic drink by the fermentation by yeast of a flavoured, sugary solution.

When yeast, a living organism, is put into a solution containing sugar and certain other essentials, it "feeds" upon the sugar to obtain the energy it needs for self-reproduction, and a by-product of the reproductive process is the alcohol we seek.

As the yeast multiplies, it converts the sugar in the liquid half to alcohol and half to gas (carbon dioxide) by weight, the gas providing the sparkle and head so much admired in a good beer.

With wines this fermentation process can continue until 15 or 16 parts in every 100 of the liquid are alcohol, at which level further yeast activity is inhibited by the alcohol, and any sugar still remaining in the wine will serve only to sweeten it.

With the ordinary beers less sugar is used, so that the final alcoholic strength may be anywhere between 3% and about 6%. By increasing the sugar content (as with wine) we can increase the strength to 8% and even 10%, so that the beer is really a "barley wine", but it should be noted that popular preference has always been for the weaker beers, since your beer drinker usually prefers quantity to strength.

The main difference between winemaking and brewing, however, lies in how the requisite sugar is obtained. In winemaking, we ferment the natural sugar of fruit juices (glucose, fructose, laevulose, etc.) or sugar which we have added to them (sucrose, glucose, etc.).

In *true* brewing (as distinct from the making of imitation beers from malt extract or ingredients other than barley) the basic material for providing the sugar is grain—in this country barley—which contains starch. Starch in its original state is not fermentable by the yeasts we wish to employ, so it has first to be converted to sugar, which *is* fermentable.

This is done by germinating the barley (malting) and steeping it in hot water or "liquor" (mashing). This sets up a chemical action which converts the starch in the malt to soluble carbohydrates, making sugar (maltose or dextrose) available for fermentation.

The wort, as the liquid is now called, is then boiled with the hops to concentrate it and improve its keeping qualities, before fermentation. Then comes any after-treatment, such as clarification (fining) and, finally, storage in barrel or bottle.

When studying the home production of beer, it is a great help to take a quick look at what happens in commercial brewing, for if we fully know the basic processes we are that much less liable to go wrong with our "home brew".

MALTING

After the barley has been cleaned, and all dust and "foreign bodies" removed, it has to be malted, or germinated. This is done in one of two ways, known as the "floor" and "drum" systems. The grain is steeped in water for two or three days and, as it absorbs moisture, swells and softens. Surplus water is drained off and, in the "floor" method, the grain is heaped on the malting floor, which is so designed as to make temperature and ventilation controllable, because as germination proceeds temperature rises, just as it does in compost heap or haystack. The malsters turn the grain by hand with shovels to ensure even malting.

The only difference in the "drum" system is that the steeped grain is malted in revolving cylinders which likewise allow for easy control of warmth and ventilation. During malting the barley germinates and a tiny shoot, the acrospire, starts to grow within from the base of the grain and a gas, carbon dioxide, is given off.

Germination and growth may continue for about 10 days, at temperatures in the 13°–17° C. range, with plenty of aeration, by which time the acrospire, still within the husk, will be about three-quarters the length of the grain. Growth of this "green malt" has then to be terminated, and this is done by kilning, a drying process. Moderate heat is employed at first, 50°–70° C. (122°–158° F.) and then the temperature is raised to wither the shoot and, perhaps, lightly or heavily roast the malt. Final temperatures are lower for pale malts (80°–85° C.) than for dark malts (over 100° C.) and it is at this stage, by delicate variations of temperature, timing and method, that different flavours can be created, and a whole range of pale, crystal, brown and black malts produced. The green malt may be kilned over wood chips, heated in an oven, or even roasted fully.

The kilning process is obviously a tricky one for the average home brewer, who can, if he wishes, buy ready malted grain and thus start with the next process which occurs in the brewery. . . .

CRACKING

The malt is then ground, or lightly crushed between rollers, and at this stage is known as "grist" (hence "grist to the mill").

MASHING

This, it must be emphasised, is the most important single operation in brewing, for it is here that the principal enzymatic change occurs in the malt. Enzymes are biological catalysts, or agencies within the grain which have power to change other substances without themselves being changed, and there are several which have all to play their part. The enzyme *cytase* dissolves the protective cellulose coating of the barley granules, giving access to the starch, which the enzyme *diastase* then liquefies and converts to fermentable sugar (or maltose), and dextrins which dissolve in the water to form a weet, malt-flavoured liquid known as "sweet wort".

Enzyme activity is extremely sensitive to temperature changes, so by varying conditions during mashing the brewer is able to vary the wort and therefore the resultant beer. The temperature in the mash tun must be between 62° and 68° C. (or 145°–155° F.).

The grist is mixed with hot water in the mash tun, and other "grits" such as flaked barley, oats or maize may be added, and the temperature of 62°–68° C. is maintained for at least two hours. During this time the principal starch-to-sugar conversion takes place.

Then the sweet wort is run off from the bottom of the mash tun and at the same time the mash is sprayed (or "sparged") from above with hot water. (In Continental brewing mashing starts at a low temperature, but quantities of the wort are taken to another vessel, brought up to boiling, and then returned to the mash tun, thus gradually raising the temperature of the whole mash. This is known as the "decoction" system, and the British method as the "infusion" one.)

BOILING

The wort is then boiled with the hops at the rate of 1 lb.–5 lb. hops per barrel of 36 gallons (a) to stabilise the wort by sterilising it and preventing further enzyme activity; (b) to concentrate it to the required strength, and (c) to extract the preservative and flavouring qualities of the hops. Since some of these are volatile and would be driven off, it is usual to add some hops towards the end of this process. Boiling also assists eventual clarification by precipitating some of the complex malt proteins. From the boiler the wort is pumped to the "hop back", another vessel with a false bottom. The hops settle on to this and form a natural filter bed, through which the hopped wort drains on its way to the coolers and fermenting vessels.

FERMENTING

It is cooled down to about 15° C. (60° F.) and run into large fermenting vessels, and the yeast is "pitched". Top-fermenting yeast is used (except for lager) and the fermentation lasts about a week; when it is completed the beer is skimmed to remove top yeast, and racked into barrels.

CONDITIONING

The cloudy draught beer (cloudy because yeast is still in suspension in it) is then "fined", or rendered brilliant, by the use of isinglass, the flocculent fragments of which settle gradually, carrying down the suspended solids and leaving the beer above brilliant. Other conditioning, such as the addition of dry (unboiled) hops to pale ales, are practised to improve flavour and aroma, and to meet public taste. Treatment of the beer at this stage varies widely. Mild ales usually leave the brewery only a few days after they have been racked, and are often sweetened (or "primed"), but bottled beers and strong beers may be stored for weeks or months, during which there may be a slow secondary fermentation. Many home brewers puzzle over how to obtain a clear bottled beer with a good head, but without yeast deposit. The brewery overcomes the problem by fining the beer, chilling it, and saturating it with carbon dioxide under pressure.

Having seen what the commercial brewers do, let us see how we can adapt their methods for use in our home. . . .

Home Brewing Ingredients

THERE is no difficulty about brewing at home nowadays, for there is on the market an abundance of home brew kits to enable one to produce a whole range of beers, from lager to extra stout. Some of them are truly excellent and produce scientifically balanced worts, giving you marvellous beers, others are abominations from which not even a master brewer could produce a decent pint. All of them, however, will be accompanied by the manufacturer's instructions, which are usually simplicity itself to follow, and if that is how you wish to brew . . . go to it. But it is by no means the cheapest or most satisfactory way, and the mere fact that you are reading this book indicates that you would like to be able to follow your own inclinations and produce your own beers much more economically.

The principal ingredients of beers and stouts are malt, hops, sugar, water and yeast, so let us look at each in more detail.

First, malt. There are three main ways open to the home brewer for producing a wort from which a convincing beer or stout may be made. These are by using:

(a) Malt (ready-malted barley)
(b) Malt extract
(c) A combination of both.

Malt can be supplemented or reinforced by the use of other grits (or grains) to supply extra starch for conversion, and a further economy is to substitute sugar in one form or another for some of the malt. This process, however, must not be carried too far or an inferior, cider-like beer with terrible hangover propensities will result.

28

A sensible combination of malt, malt extract, grits, and sugar, is probably the most easy, economical, and satisfactory solution.

MALT

Only the best barley goes for malting purposes, and malting quality commands the highest price, so farmers naturally try to produce grain of that standard. Nowadays Scandinavian hybrids, peculiarly suitable to modern harvesting methods, although they do not make good malt quite so readily, are popular; the most commonly grown variety is probably Proctor.

What does one look for in a specimen of malting barley? It should have an even grain size, it should be fully ripe (i.e. it should have a finely wrinkled skin) and should be in "good condition", sweet and dry. Internally, the grain should be floury, indicating a low nitrogen content. Once the barley has been malted, it should be think-skinned and float when put into water, and it should still be sweet in taste and smell.

Some malts on offer are of poor quality, but a good malt on mashing, at 1 lb. to the gallon, could produce a gravity of up to 1025 (a brewery might get 25% more).

Malt, like coffee, can be roasted light or dark, and is sold under various descriptions and in various forms. But the main fact to remember is that the basic malt of all brewing, from which the strength of the beer is derived, is *pale malt*, simply because this gives the highest yield.

Generally speaking, the more a malt is roasted (i.e. the darker it is) the lower its yield. Thus pale malt is employed to obtain strength, coloured malts are added in small quantities to deepen colour or alter flavour.

Coloured malts are given various names, according to their depth of colour; thus one comes across crystal, amber, caramel, brown, black and "patent black" malts. Crystal and caramel malts will have been kilned in the same way as pale malt, but afterwards roasted lightly. The content of the granule is crisp, and, used at 1 lb. per gallon, such a malt will give possibly 16 or 17 degrees of gravity, if mashing is carried out carefully. The yield is not so important as in the case of pale malt, of course, since these malts are likely to be used only to impart a more interesting colour to the beer, and need not be more than a twentieth of the total quantity of malt used; that is the commercial level. Used in large quantities, it can convey a very pleasant light and nutty flavour, as in the best bitter beers.

Amber and brown malts are similar, but slightly darker, and give a slightly deeper tone in the finished beer. The granule's contents are more powdery. These malts are useful for lending a smooth, full taste which is useful in the case of mild or brown ales.

Black malt has been much more heavily roasted, at higher temperatures, so much so that it will give a wonderful depth of colour, but its yield in terms of gravity will be low, probably not more than two or three degrees per lb. per gallon. The roasting process is a delicate one, for if the temperature is too high the malt will be burnt, but if it is too low it will not be caramelised, and the temperature has therefore to be held between the two relevant levels (440°–480° F.). Black malts give stout its burnt and rather woody taste, and in the case of sweet stouts caramel is sometimes added to give the desired smoothness and sweetness. In a stout wort the alcoholic strength, again, is derived from pale malt, three parts of which will be used to each one part of black. **"Patent black"** malt is used in well-known "extra" stouts.

All these malts, of course, have to be mashed by the home brewer to extract the flavour, but he can take a short cut and avoid even this rather tricky job by employing malt extract. Generally, the principle to remember is: the more malt, the more the body imparted finally to the drink. And the more body it has, the more it will need some bitter herb added, to counteract the heaviness and keep the palate clear.

OTHER GRITS

The starch in green malt is converted to sugar during mashing by the enzyme diastase. Diastase is sufficiently powerful to convert not only the starch of the malt, but that of any other grain (or "grit") that is added to it; a malt which has this ability to a great degree is described as "highly diastatic". We can take advantage of this and reduce the cost—or increase the strength—of our brews by including in the mash a proportion of other grits—maize, oats, rice, or wheat, but they must be cooked first.

For instance, $\frac{1}{4}$ lb. of crushed maize or ground rice, and $\frac{1}{4}$ lb. malt can be heated in $\frac{1}{2}$ gallon of water to 45° C. (113° F.) and held at this temperature for half-an-hour, then boiled for a quarter-of-an-hour. This can then be mixed with a main mash, consisting say, of 1$\frac{1}{2}$ lb. malt which has been steeped in half a gallon of water at 38° C. (100° F.) and kept at 30° C. (86° F.) for another hour. Mashing then proceeds in the usual way.

The comparative starch contents, as percentages of dry substances, in a few common "grits" are: Maize rice, 80–85; polished rice, 88–92; tapioca, 75–90; wheat, 65–78; potatoes, 65–75; oats, 60–70; rye, 60–65; and barley, 57–65. Some of these are often used to add body and strength to a thin beer. It is as well, however, to avoid this particular commercial practice, since the economy is not great and the risks of making poor beers, which do not ferment or clear well, are much increased.

MALT EXTRACT

. . . far more economical than true malt, brings within the home brewer's grasp a whole range of beers and stouts of all strengths, and obviates all the rather tedious (if interesting) work of malting and mashing.

To make quality beers, it is true, one needs to use malt in its granular form, but malt extract has the overwhelming advantage of simplicity, and there is no doubt that this is the method of brewing that the great majority of amateurs adopt.

The big disadvantage of beers made entirely from extract is that they do have a characteristic nutty flavour which is quite distinctive. Some do not find it disagreeable, but if you do, it can be minimised by using, say, 1 lb. of crystal malt or 1 lb. of roasted barley. This should be cracked with a rolling pin and boiled with the hops. For darker beers and stouts the addition of roasted malt is essential.

All the home brewer has to do is to infuse his hops or other herbs in boiling water, and then pour the boiling liquid over his malt extract, plus any sugar which he uses for reasons of economy. Light ales can be made in this way at ridiculously little cost, as low as 2p a pint, and even very strong brews need cost only 2½p a pint.

Malt extract varies greatly in quality, and if you buy it from a chemist be sure that you get a pure extract and not one flavoured with cod liver oil! Some extracts on the market impart an unpleasant bitter taste, a bitterness unlike that of beer, and generally it is advisable to go to a reliable home-brew supplies firm to obtain an extract of assured brewing quality.

Nowadays some excellent brands, as supplied to the trade, are available to the amateur, containing the right sugar balance for the production of body and alcohol, the right protein balance for good clearing and head retention, freedom from bacterial infection which could cause off flavours, and a standardised low colour, so that the home brewer can "tint up" to his own requirements.

Extract is usually sold in 2 lb. tins or jars, but is naturally cheaper if purchased in 14 lb., 28 lb., or 56 lb. lots. It may be a little stiff, but if the jar is stood in a warm place for a few hours or in hot water for a few minutes the extract proves easier to pour. If you wet your free hand with cold water you will be able to handle the ribbon of malt without it sticking to your fingers. The jar should be rinsed out with really hot water to remove the last of the extract.

The extract can also be purchased in convenient liquid and dry powder form; you can obtain a dark dried extract or a liquid black caramelised one for making stout.

HOPS AND HERBS

The part which hops play in the production of quality beer is all-important, for they affect both flavour and keeping qualities.

Normally one-third to 1 oz. of hops (the dried cones which carry the seeds of the female hop plant, *Humulus Lupulus*) are used to the gallon, but on occasion as much as 2¼ oz. may be necessary. The chemistry of the hop and its influence on the brew is complicated, but it is sufficient here to say that the hop contributes three main things: volatile oils, giving aroma and flavour; resins, giving bitterness and improving the keeping qualities of the beer, and tannin-like constituents which make for brilliance.

Originally, the second function was the most important, i.e. hops were regarded mainly as a preservative, but nowadays the first function takes eminence, since the bitter flavour of hops has come to be appreciated and expected in a beer. The bitterness of a brew can be adjusted by increasing or decreasing the amount of hops used. The more hops, the more bitter the finished drink. High quality pale ales and bitter beers are heavily hopped, mild ales and stouts usually less so, and lagers least of all. Generally speaking, more hops are employed in this country than in Continental breweries.

The hop, with its delicate, fresh flavour (when used in small amounts) is the natural partner to malt; its bitterness, even when strong, is never disagreeable. Moreover, in an age of "tranquillisers", it should be recognised as a natural soporific (the "hop pillow" is an old remedy) and sleep comes easily after hopped beer.

Hops for use in beer should be fresh and odorous, and leave a stickiness on the palms of the hands if rubbed. At one time the only hops the home brewer could purchase were dried, compressed ones, or those of doubtful vintage from a chemist. Now, however, it is possible to buy named varieties in exactly the same way as the trade does, either through a home brew firm or from a hop merchant in London (most of them are in the East End). Home brewing clubs could very well purchase in bulk for their members, since no trader will welcome being asked for a few ounces at a time!

The hop used does have a tremendous influence upon the flavour, character, and head retention of a beer, so it is important to use the best. Experimenting with different varieties, and with blends, can be both stimulating and rewarding.

Most of the following are now available:

Fuggle: A Kentish hop which has been used for over one hundred years, and which is probably still the favourite of the brewing industry. Strong-flavoured, and therefore useful in the stronger-flavoured beers such as mild and brown ales. **W.V.G.s** and **Bramling Cross** are similar.

33

Golding: Named after a Kentish grower who established the strain over 160 years ago, this hop is lighter in flavour, and is best used in light ales, best bitters, and beers of that type. Excellent for dry hopping if so desired.

Northern Brewer: A markedly bitter hop, so much so that 2 oz. is enough for 4½ or 5 gallons: excellent in stouts.

Bullion: An American variety noted for its outstanding bitterness. Its strength of flavour is such that it can really only be used in conjunction with other hops, but is particularly valuable in stouts, or particularly bitter beers, and in beers which are to have a long maturation period.

Hallertauer: A Bavarian hop which is now being imported and from which noble beers can be brewed. Particularly useful in light, grain-malt beers.

Saaz: Another imported hop which is ideal for the making of lager, since it has a delicate, dry flavour and not too pronounced an aroma.

Other varieties which may be encountered and occasionally purchased include: Bramling, Brewer's Favourite, Brewer's Gold, College Cluster, Concord, Copper Hop, Defender, Density, Early Bird, Early Choice, Malling, Midseason, OF/27, Pride of Kent, Quality and Sun Shine.

It is quite easy to grow your own hops, and in this way to be sure of having the correct varieties. A nurseryman will supply rooted sets which are planted out just as one would plant, say, a rose tree, the distance apart depending on the height of the wirework or trellis they will be trained upon; they must have air and sun to ripen. The vines will make some 25 ft. of growth a year and will require adequate support.

Choose preferably a wilt-tolerant type such as W.V.G.s, Bramling Cross, or Early Bird.

OTHER HERBS

Although the hop is now pre-eminent, other herbs can be used to impart both flavour and bitterness, and for centuries were, and it is well worth-while to experiment with them. Spruce oil, for instance. It is also a good preservative (and combines well with hops) but, unlike hops, will dispel drowsiness rather than create it. Consequently, spruce beer, with its clean, fresh flavour, will challenge any conventional beer as a refresher. It is still popular in Scandinavia, and was popular in this country less than a couple of centuries ago, as our legislation shows.

Nettles were once used in making stouts. An infusion of nettle is slightly salty (a requirement in stouts) and if nettle is used it will need plenty of hops or the roughness of black malt to give it an edge and make it palatable. Salt gives beer, like coffee, a "roundness" of flavour, but as soon as the salty taste becomes perceptible it is unpleasant, and the characteristic clean after-taste of beer is lost.

Other old-time flavourings were ginger, dandelion, burdock or sarsaparilla, and one can experiment with these—to find stimulating variations upon the more usual hop theme. Once the principle of balancing sweetness against bitterness is understood it becomes easy.

SUGARS

In brewing the term "sugar" has a special meaning, for it covers anything which can be a source of sugar, or starch, whether malt, barley, maize, rice, or any other ingredient used in beer. Here, however, we are employing the word in its more normal sense. Some of the sugar necessary in home brewing may come from malt, but generally it will be found too expensive to obtain in this way all the sugar necessary for a strong, or even a reasonably strong, brew; consequently additional sugar will be needed. This can be added by means of ordinary white household sugar (sucrose), either cane or beet (chemically they are identical).

In Bavaria, incidentally, this is illegal, for German law recognises as beer only a drink made from malt, hops, and water; no other sugar must be employed. This has not been the case in breweries in this country since 1880 and the home brewer will certainly not wish to circumscribe himself in this way, when by adding sugar he can make beer far stronger than that normally on sale.

Relatively small additions of white household sugar or sucrose for the purposes of economy will not affect the flavour of your brew, but too much sugar, rather than extract or malt, will produce a thin but overstrong beer, poor head retention—and probably a hangover! White household sugar is best for pale light-bodied beers, while *brown, moist* sugar, which is cheap, will make a darker beer, heavier in body though no stronger. It may, however, slightly affect the taste.

Invert sugar which is added to brewery wort before it is hopped and boiled, in order to increase its fermentability, undoubtedly ferments quickest of all, and can now be purchased. When yeast sets to work on sucrose, it first splits it into its two main components, glucose and fructose, or "inverts" it, making a sugar which is then speedily fermentable. Thus, by using invert, the fermentation is enabled to get away more speedily, since the yeast does not have first to effect the inversion.

If you use invert sugar (which is slightly more expensive than sucrose) note that since it contains more water it will be necessary to substitute 1¼ lb. for every 1 lb. of household sugar specified in recipes. It certainly makes a dry beer of real quality.

Invert sugar can be made quite easily as follows: Put 8 lb. ordinary sugar (sucrose, i.e. cane or beet) in a large pan with two pints of water and half a teaspoonful of citric or tartaric acid. Heat this mixture until it boils, stirring occasionally with a wooden spoon until the sugar has been dissolved. Boil gently for half an hour or so, cool, and add about two pints of water to give a total volume of exactly one gallon. One pint of this syrup contains one pound of invert sugar.

Honey was undoubtedly the form of sweetening used in many of the now-neglected herbal beers, since it is the oldest known form of sugar, and it can be substituted pound for pound for sugar in all recipes. The only precaution is that it should be boiled for 10–15 minutes in part of the water to kill unwanted bacteria which might attack the beer and turn it sour.

Glucose is now available to the home brewer and is an ideal material, for it ferments well and quickly. Best purchased in the form of honey-coloured glucose chippings (lump form) which will impart both smoothness and a trace of colour to the beer.

Liquorice, a herb, is sweet to the taste, and can be useful for taking the harshness off a stout, but it should be avoided in finer beers, of which it will spoil the clean taste. It does give the illusion of added body and sweetness, plus a peculiar pungency of its own, but all it has in fact done is to coat the tongue.

Caramel, the commercial name for what used to be called *burnt sugar*, is most useful in brewing as a general colourant, and by its aid brews can be easily tinted from a light brown to a really dark colour, depending upon the quantity used. It can be purchased as liquid gravy browning, which sounds peculiar, but it will be seen from the label that this is in fact caramel. The amount to be used varies from a teaspoonful in three gallons for bitter to a tablespoon for a dark brown, and it is added at the boiling stage.

Caramel can be made thus: Put a dessertspoonful of white sugar into half a pint of water; bring to boiling. Do not stir. Lower gas or heat and let syrup simmer till it turns to white candy; then stir slowly. The syrup will gradually turn a light brown colour; keep stirring until the caramel is nearly black. Then remove from gas and put on approximately half a pint of cold water. Bring this slowly to the boil, stirring all the time until caramel is completely dissolved.

Lactose, the milk sugar that is added to what was once called "milk stout" (the name is no longer used nowadays, since it was held to be misleading, implying the inclusion of milk in the beer) is not fermentable by usual brewing yeasts, and therefore, if used, will remain in the drink simply as sweetening. It is useful for this purpose, and can be added to a stout, or other beer, at the rate of 3-4 ozs. to the gallon. Lactose can be purchased from most chemists.

As a rough guide to the amount of sugar to be used, one can say most beers will require between ½ lb. and 1 lb. of malt, or malt extract, and possibly, in addition, up to ¾ lb. of sugar per gallon.

WATER

It is not accidental that the best beers in Britain are brewed at Burton-on-Trent, that Hampshire is famous for its bitter, or that Ireland is renowned for her stouts and porters, for the brewing of particular beers was once very much a matter of the composition of the water in the locality. High quality pale ales and bitter beers such as produced at Burton-on-Trent demand the type of water which occurs there naturally, water containing a comparatively high proportion of gypsum, or calcium sulphate. This helps one to attain clarity in the finished beer because it aids the separation of certain nitrogenous elements in the malt, which can be filtered off with the spent hops.

It has been said that to be ideal for bitters such water should contain 21 grains per gallon of calcium sulphate and 7 grains per gallon of magnesium sulphate. Chlorides are not essential.

If you live in a soft water district you can obtain the desired effect by adding to the gallon up to 1 level teaspoon of the chemical which can be purchased quite cheaply from a chemist, or from brewing supplies firms under the name of "water treatment". Ask for calcium sulphate, gypsum, or plaster of Paris.

Mild ales and stouts and the best lagers, on the other hand, are made with soft water, often described as "London type", containing a fair amount of calcium and magnesium carbonate and a certain amount of chlorides. If you intend to make these regularly, and live in a hard water district, the installation of a water softener is an obvious advantage. The addition of a teaspoon of salt to each four gallons will help. You can also buy a "water treatment" for this purpose. Sulphate brings out a dry flavour as in pale ales, chloride a fuller one, as in stouts.

Generally, however, it will pay you to make the type of drink best made with your local water, soft or hard.

YEAST

Baker's yeast (1 oz. to the gallon) is not really very satisfactory for beer because it does not settle down into a firm sediment and will rise in clouds in the beer at the slightest movement of a jar or bottle or when a screw stopper is removed. Racking is difficult and undue wastage is caused. For the occasional experimental gallon, however, ordinary granulated baker's yeast may be used and will produce a satisfactory beer, if you do not mind wasting a little in this way. A level teaspoon to the gallon will suffice.

Most breweries have their own favourite strains of *saccharomyces cerevisiae*, which do have some effect upon the character of their finished products, and if you are lucky you can sometimes obtain a jar from your local brewery. Such a yeast is naturally excellent for your purpose, for it will already have a pronounced beery flavour, and once you have some, if you are brewing weekly, you will always have an ample supply, and probably an almost embarrassing surplus. I once kept one such brewery yeast continually in use for over two years. At that time I was brewing weekly in glass jars and all that was necessary, after racking one brew into half gallon bottles, was to throw out two-thirds of the lees, leaving just sufficient to fill the peripheral groove at the bottom of the jar. The new wort was then siphoned in on top of this and fermentation would begin immediately.

Brewery yeasts, it should be noted, are usually top fermenting varieties, and this often involves some skimming, for a thick "cake" of yeast will form and float on the surface of the beer. I find that the particular top yeast which I most commonly use produces a real mat of yeast on the surface of the beer, so much so that skimming is always necessary every two days or so.

The initial scum and surplus yeast should be skimmed off, but once a creamy foam appears—the so-called "cauliflower head" or "rocky head", do not skim again until you are going to bottle.

The surplus yeast, of course, provides an excellent starter for the next brew, but there is always far too much, and quantities have to be thrown away.

If the head is not skimmed in this way it will eventually fall to the bottom and impart to the beer a flavour called by brewers "yeast-bitten". Great attention must be paid, when using a top-fermenting yeast, to this point.

Most home brewers, we feel, may wish to avoid this problem, and can do so by using a reliable bottom-fermenting yeast such as is commonly supplied.

You can also make a starter bottle from the dregs of a bottle of your favourite bottled beer! Allow the bottle to stand undisturbed for two or three days, then pour off your drinks, leaving a couple of inches of beer behind, containing any yeast which may be in that particular bottle. Make up a solution of $\frac{1}{4}$ pint of hot water, 1 teaspoon of sugar, 1 teaspoon of malt extract and a lump of citric acid the size of a pea and, when it is cool, pour it into the beer bottle, plug it with cotton wool and stand it in a warm place, such as the airing cupboard. If you are lucky (it depends largely on what type of beer or stout you are using) you will get a vigorous fermentation which can be used as a starter for your next brew. Several of the better known bottled beers can be used in this way and one which is rarely found to fail is Worthington White Label. The dregs of a bottle of home brew, of course, make an excellent starter for a following brew, because there is much more yeast sediment in a bottle of home brew than in a bottle of commercial beer. So once you have acquired a tiny amount of true brewer's yeast you need never be without ample supplies, indeed you are eventually likely to have so much that you will be throwing quantities away every time you bottle.

But at first you will probably plump for a good sedimentary ale or lager yeast, a "bottom fermenter", which will settle down firmly and allow the clear beer to be siphoned off. Although such ale and lager yeasts may be more expensive initially, they are not really much more so, since they can be used over and over again, either by the above method, or by using them from a "starter bottle" or wort. Only two-thirds of this is used and the remaining third topped up with a little malt extract, sugar and water to keep it going.

The use of a good vitamin yeast food to boost the action of the yeast is most important in brewing, since a quick, vigorous fermentation is required. Malt itself is a nutrient, of course, but your extract may not contain all the trace minerals essential to good yeast growth. Nowadays such energisers can be bought so cheaply that it is hardly worth bothering to make up your own, and they are added to the wort either as a powder or as a tablet, which is first crushed. One teaspoonful of citric acid to four or five gallons will help create a healthy brew, and preclude off flavours which sometimes occur in its absence. Often when a wort refuses to ferment, the addition of a trace of acid will do the trick.

PRINCIPLES TO REMEMBER

Finally, excellent brewing principles to remember are:
1. The more malt, the more body and strength.
2. The more body, the more hops needed.
3. The more hops, the greater the bitterness.
4. The more sugar, the greater the strength.
5. The sooner bottled, the greater the head (and risk!)

STRENGTH

And now, quite early in this book, may I sound a warning?
DO NOT MAKE YOUR BEER TOO STRONG.

At first sight this may appear to be extraordinary advice.
"Surely the whole point of brewing my own beer," you may
well ask, "is that by so doing I can have a better beer than
I can buy?" And "better", for most people, is at first synonymous with "stronger".

But strength is even less the principal criterion of a good
beer than it is of a good wine.

After all, the extra strength is easy enough to achieve; one
has merely to use more malt or sugar, and ferment for a
longer period, and it is quite feasible to produce a beer of,
say, wine strength, up to 10–14% alcohol by volume.

But is it desirable? Breweries will tell you that their
strongest beers are by no means the most popular, and the
answer does not lie simply in the fact that they are more
expensive. The most popular beer in Britain is the weakest—
mild.

Why is this? Surely the answer lies in the beer drinker's
approach to his drinking. The beer drinker, unlike the wine
lover, expects to be able to drink a fair quantity, say three or
four pints, without ill effect; it should make him pleasantly
relaxed, but not make him drunk, or leave him with a splitting
headache the following day.

Any beer drinker who has had an "evening out" drinking
a high gravity (i.e. strong, quality beer) will know what I
mean! That is why your habitual beer drinker prefers the
lower-gravity bitters and milds; he can drink them for a
whole evening's darts without risk.

Surely the same is true of home brewed beer? It is neither
wise nor hospitable to brew beer so strong that after two

glasses your friend slips under the table or has a severe headache next day; he will not thank you for it! Home brewed beers are not a whit inferior to commercial ones, but they are often made far too strong, with disastrous results upon host or guest, and it is this which earns them a quite undeserved bad reputation.

Therefore aim at making your brews of roughly the same strength as the principal commercial types you are emulating and do not fall into the error of making them so *very* much too strong. If you *must* produce double-strength beer, or "barley wine", then please, please, treat it with respect, warn your friends of its strength, and serve it in smaller glasses, as publicans do their "nips" and "specials", and NOT in pint glasses or tankards.

YOU HAVE BEEN WARNED!

OBTAINING A HEAD

One of the principal difficulties which amateur brewers encounter is that of obtaining a good head, which does so much to make a home-brew look attractive. The problem is akin to that of producing a sparkling, as opposed to a still, wine. It is easy, by bottling prematurely, to produce a beer with a foaming, uncontrollable head, far more suitable for extinguishing fires than topping a tankard. It is also easy, by bottling too late, and adding no priming sugar, to produce a beer which is as strong as the sugar used allows, but flat.

The secret is to ferment the beer almost to completion and then, when bottling, to add *just enough* priming sugar to produce a sparkle and head.

One can also solve the problem by adding to a flat beer a "heading liquid" which can be purchased from suppliers, with full instructions, but this, while it gives an artificial head, does not seem to impart "life" to the beer, and is therefore not so satisfactory.

If head retention is poor it is probably the fault of poor quality malt (or using insufficient) or of not having allowed the beer to mature.

CARBONATION

A modern development is that one can now buy devices for carbonating small quantities of beer—usually in 7-pint cans—or for maintaining the carbonation of a larger quantity say four or five gallons. Sparklet bulbs are used to inject CO_2 under pressure.

SEDIMENT

Another perennial problem, allied with the foregoing, is that of obtaining a beer free of yeast sediment. This is virtually impossible, because if one is to have a slight fermentation in the bottle, as mentioned above, there must obviously always be a slight yeast deposit as a result. If you are *very* particular, you can do as some home brewers do and invert the bottles to allow the yeast to settle on the stopper, and then (over a sink!) gently partially release it and quickly re-screw it home, so that the pressure blows the yeast sediment out.

But, since home-brew is so cheap, this would appear to be rather wasted effort; if you feel so very aesthetic, it is far easier to use a pewter tankard. The beer will taste better and what the eye does not see . . . !

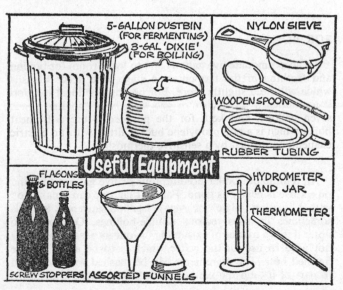

5-GALLON DUSTBIN (FOR FERMENTING) 3-GAL 'DIXIE' (FOR BOILING)

NYLON SIEVE

WOODEN SPOON

RUBBER TUBING

FLAGONS & BOTTLES

SCREW STOPPERS

ASSORTED FUNNELS

HYDROMETER AND JAR

THERMOMETER

Useful Equipment

Equipment you will need

SINCE beer, obviously, is drunk in larger quantities than wine, by the tumbler, half-pint, or pint, one naturally tends to brew in greater bulk, and, whilst one can still make experimental single gallons, most home brewers eventually come round to the idea of making four or five gallons at a time. This is about the largest quantity that a man can comfortably lift; ladies may have to be content with 2½ or 3 gallons!

FOR BOILING

To accommodate five gallons and to leave room for boiling and frothing in the fermentation stage, one needs utensils which will hold slightly more. For boiling, the ideal solution is undoubtedly an electric or gas wash boiler holding about seven gallons, and kept for the purpose. I use a Bruheat boiler which is a polypropylene bucket fitted with an electric element, controlled by a sensitive thermostat.

An aluminium boiler holding four or five gallons to stand on a stove is nearly as good. Failing that, one can "make do" with a 3-gallon "dixie" or even a 1-gallon saucepan, but this sometimes involves tedious double-boilings. One point to note: if it is a matter of extracting flavour into water one does not need to use *all* the water which is to be added to the finished beer. The ingredients can be mashed with or boiled in part of it and the balance added, cold, later. Galvanised

44

boilers, incidentally, are safe enough for boiling up an infusion of grain or herbs, but should not be used once any acid has been included, or there may be a risk of metal poisoning.

For infusing hops a hop bag, made of muslin and with a long string, is useful. The hops can be boiled in this and are thus easily removed before fermenting begins. Another useful item is a rubber siphoning tube (from any chemist, about 8p).

FOR MASHING

When making a beer or stout from malt or other grain there are two methods of mashing which you can follow. If you decide to mash the malt as the brewery does you will need an outer vessel with a tap fitted at the bottom, and a smaller vessel with a perforated bottom to fit inside it. These two will comprise your mash tun. I use a stoneware jar with a bottom tap for the outer vessel, and a 1½-gallon polythene bucket with 100 ⅛-in. holes drilled all over the bottom for the inner one, but you could also use the top portion of a steamer, which has a suitably perforated base.

For mashing by the simplified process which is also detailed on page 59 you will need a 2-gallon polythene bucket or other container, with some form of lid or cover. For this system you will also need a 50-watt immersion heater, with or without thermostat. For larger quantities, use a Bruheat boiler, as described on pp. 61 and 62.

Whichever container you use for mashing, it is a good idea to have a well fitted lid or some form of cover, to retain heat.

And a thermometer (5° to boiling point, costing about 90p) is indispensable.

FOR FERMENTING

For fermenting and general use in brewing the ideal vessel is one of the light, easily cleaned, polythene brewbins to be obtained from most chain stores and costing £2.50. They last well, and hold five, seven or eleven gallons. It is preferable to buy a white brewbin as some of the colourants in the coloured bins are toxic. If you have a coloured bin use a soft polythene liner to be on the safe side. Easily handled, they are a joy to use. One can also ferment, of course, in glass 5-gallon carboys, under a fermentation lock, but skimming and foam control is rendered more difficult and one cannot handle carboys with the same care-free assurance that one can a plastic brewbin Do not use any metal containers for fermenting, and avoid old lead-glaze red earthenware crocks, which may have a poisonous or faulty glaze.

Using the "open" container, skim the brew once or twice; using the "closed" one this is not possible and it may prove desirable in this case to reduce the quantity of hops used, or the brew may be unduly bitter, since much of the bitterness seems to be concentrated in the first "head", or "corona" which forms.

For small quantities a 2-gallon polythene bucket, particularly if marked inside with liquid measures, is useful. Do not fiddle about in beer brewing with 1-pint or quart measures: a 1-gallon measure such as a saucepan or glass jar will save a lot of time. But be sure that the glass jar *does* hold eight pints: some hold nine.

FOR EASY HANDLING

Make yourself a trolley from a rectangle of ½-inch wood —I used marine ply—with a castor fixed under each corner, so that it stands 2 or 3 inches high. Your brewbin or primary fermenter stands on this and the wort can easily be run into it from your boiler's tap. Such a trolley makes it possible to move a 5-gallon (or even bigger) brew with ease.

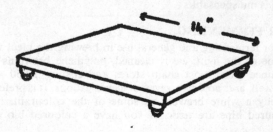

FOR STRAINING

Straining of small quantities is best done with a large nylon flour sieve, easy to use and clean, but if you are dealing regularly with big quantities of hops, and grain or bran, it will pay you to make a wooden "picture-frame" crisscrossed by tape or cord, to fit the top of your vessel. On this it is then a simple plan to lay a piece of muslin, and the whole mash can be tipped out in one go and left to drain, instead of having to be strained a little at a time.

FOR SIPHONING

. . . a "floating siphon". Use an 8-inch square of ½-inch wood as a float, fitting a short glass tube through it and attaching your rubber siphon tube to the top of this. Underneath fit a 1½-inch leg of dowel to each corner. As you rack, the siphon float will sink down on the surface of the brew but at the end the lees will remain virtually undisturbed because of the legs.

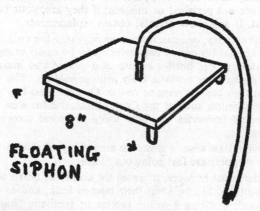

FLOATING
SIPHON

FOR STORAGE

One-gallon glass jars with ear handles, and fitted with fermentation lock, as now widely used in winemaking, are always handy for the odd gallon and can usually be obtained from restaurants and grocers on payment of 13p or so, or from the trade at slightly greater cost.

Your most important containers, however, are the bottles in which the finished beer is to be stored, and for this quart, thick-glass beer or cider flagons should be collected — you will need 16 or 17, since you will probably be making beer four gallons at a time.

You can either retain them when you buy bottled beer at your "local", and thus gradually amass the number you need, or you can buy two dozen or so outright at an off-licence, wine shop or public house.

These strong and safe bottles are virtually indispensable if you wish to make an attractive, sparkling beer with a good "head", so they are a good investment.

Reject any which are cracked, or which have chips around the neck or base, making the bottle weak at that point and leading to a risk of its exploding as pressure builds up within it. The pressure in a beer bottle is as great as that in a car tyre!

If they have screw-stoppers, make sure that their rubber rings are not perished or missing; if they are, your beer will go flat. If any show defects, obtain replacements.

Alternatively, one can nowadays buy from brewing supplies firms special tin crown caps which can be easily crimped on to ordinary beer bottles by use of a simple and inexpensive tool, giving your bottle a truly professional air. The trouble is that they are not easy to re-use. One can also buy push-in plastic closures such as the Continentals use for wine bottles and some breweries are now using to reseal crown-closed bottles.

It would be wise to invest in something of this sort, since screw stoppers are fast going out of use.

Some home brewers, to avoid the chores of bottle washing and bottling, like to keep their beer in bulk, and to do this one needs a strong 4-gallon tap jar or synthetic "barrel".

For beers, bottles and jars are infinitely preferable to casks, which produce most disappointing results, so much so that they are not really worth considering. Inside three or four days the brew will be flat, since the gas escapes through the wood; moreover beer casks are much more difficult to maintain in good condition.

For measuring sugar content —the hydrometer

Finally—buy a hydrometer.

Many people fight shy of the hydrometer, but in beer-making it is virtually a necessity, for it can tell you, with certainty, exactly when it is safe to bottle, thus avoiding dangerous explosions later which may result if you bottle by guesswork. With heavy beers, using up to 2 lb. of malt and/or sugar to the gallon, you can bottle when the S.G. is below 1010, with light beers, using up to 1 lb. per gallon, when the S.G. is below 1005.

But it has other uses: with its aid you can calculate reasonably accurately the right amount of malt and/or sugar to produce a beer of any specified strength, thus removing the guesswork from your brewing. Before mashing grain malt you can test your malt and know what gravity you can hope to achieve with a particular batch of malt; minor adjustments can be made to the prepared wort by means of sugar. You can also check upon the progress of a fermentation.

The word hydrometer means "water-measurer" but it is more accurately called a saccharometer, or "sugar measurer", for its basic purpose is to discover how much sugar there is in the wort. Fermentation uses up the sugar to produce alcohol and carbon dioxide; therefore if we can discover how much sugar is used up during a ferment, we can calculate exactly how much alcohol has been produced, and how strong the resultant beer is.

The more sugar there is in a liquid, the thicker or denser it will become, or the greater its gravity will be. The better, too, it will support anything floating in it; the hydrometer makes use of this principle. To measure different gravities, we naturally need a scale of some sort, and an obvious and convenient standard from which to start is that of water. Water is therefore given the arbitrary gravity of 1.000, other liquids are compared specifically with this, and the resultant figures are said to be their **specific gravities.**

Thus, liquids heavier than water (or, in our case, containing more sugar) may have **specific gravities** such as 1.050, 1.120 or 1.117 degrees. When talking of gravities, however, we omit the first "1" and the decimal point. Therefore the **specific** gravities quoted are exactly the same as gravities of 50, 120 and 117 respectively.

For brewing you will need a hydrometer covering the range 1.000 to 1.100.

The hydrometer is a glass tube (with a bulbous lower end containing the scale, and it is weighted at the bottom so that it will float upright in a liquid. The reading is taken where the level of the main surface of the liquid would cut the scale.

The thinner the liquid (the less its gravity) the deeper the hydrometer will sink in it; the denser the liquid (the greater its gravity) the higher the hydrometer will float, and the more the scale will protrude above the surface.

Therefore the scale of figures in the hydrometer is "upside down", the smallest being at the top and the largest at the bottom. In water, of course, the hydrometer will float with the 1.000 mark level with the surface; as you add sugar so the hydrometer will rise in the liquid. If, on the other hand, you add instead to the water a liquid **lighter** than water—alcohol, for instance—the hydrometer will sink **below** 1.000.

To use your hydrometer pour some of the wort to be assessed into a hydrometer jar. Spin the hydrometer to get rid of air bubbles clinging to its side, which can seriously affect the reading, and then, when the hydrometer is still, take the reading, with the eye at surface level.

Having obtained the reading, you can then check with the table as to whether your wort is of the correct strength, or whether any sugar needs to be added to bring it up to the desired potential strength, but it is as well not to add all the sugar at this stage. Leave a margin so that the wort can be readjusted after boiling. Rough guide: 2½ oz. of sugar will raise the gravity of a gallon by roughly five degrees; 1 lb. of sugar added to one gallon will raise the S.G. by about 35.

The hydrometer does simplify matters; after making up the wort, check the specific gravity to see how much total sugar it contains. It is then simple, with the aid of the following table, to calculate how much sugar, if any, needs to be

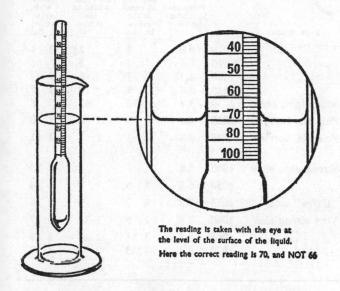

The reading is taken with the eye at the level of the surface of the liquid.

Here the correct reading is 70, and NOT 66

added, to attain exactly a wort of any desired gravity. Thus, if you wish to make a beer of 7 per cent (1055) and your wort shows a gravity of 1040, you will need to raise the gravity by 15 degrees (1055 less 1040) and reference to the table will show that you will need to add 5 oz. of sugar to the gallon to obtain that result (i.e. to reach S.G. of 1055).

With very strong beers, it is advisable to add half the sugar at the outset of fermentation, and the remainder after the first three days or the fermentation may stick. With strong, average, or weak beers this is not necessary.

Sugar in the table below, of course, means sugar and/or malt.

Type of Brew	S.G.	Potential % alcohol by vol.	Amount of sugar in the gallon lb. oz.		Amount of sugar added to the gallon lb. oz.		Vol. of one gallon with sugar added gal. fl. oz	
	1010	0.9		2		2½	1	1
	1015	1.6		4		5	1	3
	1020	2.3		7		8	1	5
	1025	3.0		9		10	1	7
Mild, light, lager	1030	3.7		12		13	1	8
Pale ale, bottled	1035	4.4		15	1	0	1	10
Pale ale, porter	1040	5.1	1	1	1	2	1	11
Strong ales, stout	1045	5.8	1	3	1	4	1	13
„ „ „	1050	6.5	1	5	1	7	1	14
"Extra" stout	1055	7.2	1	7	1	9	1	16
Very strong ales	1060	7.8	1	9	1	11	1	17
„ „ „	1065	8.6	1	11	1	14	1	19
„ „ „	1070	9.2	1	13	2	1	1	20

It is interesting to compare the strengths in the third column above with those of other drinks, e.g.: Claret 9.7%, Chateauneuf du Pape 12.5%, Champagne 13.5%, sherry 18.9%, port 20.2% and whisky 40%.

Do not forget that hydrometers are designed to be read when the liquid is at 59° F., and if it is at any other temperature you should allow for it as in the table opposite. Omit the "decimal point" of the specific gravity and make the correction to the last of its four figures. Example: A hydrometer reading of 1140 at 86° F. should be corrected to 1143.4.

Temperature		Correction
°C.	°F.	
10	50	Subtract 0.6
15	59	Correct
20	68	Add 0.9
25	77	Add 2
30	86	Add 3.4
35	95	Add 5
40	104	Add 6.8

A typical record of the progress of a fermentation:

Initial S.G. of wort before adding yeast				..	1040
S.G. after 1 days	..	..	..	..	1034
,, ,, 2 days	..	..	..	..	1023
,, ,, 3 days	..	..	..	..	1011
,, ,, 4 days	..	..	..	..	1006
,, ,, 5 days	..	..	..	..	1003
,, ,, 6 days	..	..	..	..	1001
,, ,, 7 days	..	..	..	..	1000

To calculate the final strength of the beer write down (omitting the decimal point) the S.G. at the start of the fermentation after the sugar has been added. Subtract from it the final S.G., and divide the answer by 7.36; that is the percentage of alcohol by volume in your beer or stout.

Thus:

Initial S.G	..	..	1040
Final S.G.	..	..	1000
	Difference		40

$$40 \div 7.36 = 5.4\%$$

so this particular brew is nearly $5\frac{1}{2}\%$ alcohol by volume. If you wish your next brew stronger, add more malt or sugar; weaker, use less.

Sometimes a fermentation will "stick" at 1015–1020. The best plan then is to aerate it by pouring it from one vessel to another and stirring vigorously with an oak stick. Adding fresh yeast often helps, so does a rise in temperature of a few degrees.

But if you cannot get the gravity down those last few degrees (to 1010 or below) and are in a hurry to bottle, you can always reduce the gravity by adding more water.

It is important to study carefully the time at which to bottle, for if you do so too early the fermentation will continue vigorously in the bottle, with the inevitable result—an explosion (did you know that there is as much pressure inside a commercial beer bottle as there is in the average car tyre?). Yet a slight fermentation in the bottle is desirable to give a head, and sparkle in the beer.

The hydrometer is a fairly accurate guide to when to bottle, and is therefore your greatest safeguard. Ideally, when the gravity has dropped to five or below the moment is approaching, and the lower the gravity is allowed to drop, the better, as long as there are still signs of activity in the beer. But *never* bottle until the gravity is below 10, or you may have a burst bottle. If you have no hydrometer, watch the surface of the brew, and you will notice that as the fermentation nears its end the bubbles collect in a ring centrally, and that the surface (which is cloudy when the yeast is working vigorously) is beginning to clear, since the yeast is beginning to sink down through the brew. *Now* is the time to bottle.

True Beers and Stouts

To obtain the most authentic beer, "true" beer, there is no doubt that one must do as the brewery does, and use malt, which is now readily obtainable from home brewing supplies shops. It is significant that in almost all the beer competitions which take place at national and regional level it is grain beers that feature prominently in the prize lists.

To carry the argument to its logical conclusion, anyone who is fortunate enough to have a holiday in Bavaria, and has an opportunity of sampling the beers there, where even the use of sugar is forbidden by law, will appreciate what a true "malt and hops" aroma should be.

Any home brewer worth his salt will certainly want to try his hand at "true" beers, even if he does subsequently, for convenience, turn to the employment of malt extract.

Some home brewers do try malting their own barley, but it is a tricky process and the chances of success are extremely small. It is far better to find a reliable supplier and purchase good-quality, ready-kilned malt, remembering that the bulk of the malt you will use should be *pale* malt, and that other malts are required mainly only for colouring. In mild and brown beers they will be used in quite small proportions and at the most, as when making a stout, will only be a quarter of the total malt used. The really dark malts, of course, contribute hardly any sugar at all.

When devising one's own recipes using grain malt it is essential to know how much maltose is likely to be obtained from any particular batch, since malts can vary enormously.

55

This, if one is using a mixture of grains, can be somewhat complicated, since a series of tests and a proportion calculation will be required. The simplest plan is to work on the basis that the bulk of the malt used will be pale malt—as it will—and ignore the contribution to specific gravity made by the small amounts of other grain malts included for colouring or flavouring purposes.

One does certainly need to assess the potential of the pale malt, however, and it is simplest to do this so as to arrive at a result in terms of the gravity produced by the use of 1 lb. of malt per gallon. Having discovered this, it is a matter of simple multiplication to decide how much malt per gallon one needs to use to arrive at any desired original gravity.

MALT TEST

A simple test will obviate wasting hours of time in perhaps fruitless mashing. Take 2 oz. of your crushed pale malt and put it into a saucepan, add half a pint of water heated to 155° F., and hold the temperature as nearly as possible at 150° F. for an hour. Add a further half a pint of water at the same temperature and then allow to cool to just above 60° F. Strain through a coarse filter and check the specific gravity with your hudrometer. This will give the gravity resulting from the use of 1 lb. of that particular malt to the gallon. If your test, for instance, produces a gravity of 30, each ounce contributes roughly 2 degrees of gravity (30÷16). From this it is easy to calculate how much malt will be required to be certain of reaching the gravity you desire. Any malt, incidentally, which produces a gravity of less than 23 in this test is not really worth using.

CRACKING

Before you can mash it, your malt must be cracked, to render the starch freely available, and it should be noted that "cracked" means what it says, i.e. crushed, rather than ground to a fine flour, which will make clarification difficult. If the husks can be left whole they later form a natural filter bed. So a device which will grind or crack only coarsely is required. I find a hand coffee mill of the old fashioned type an ideal tool, but one can also use a rolling pin, a bottle, or a slow-speed electric "juicer".

CRACKING MALT

A WINE BOTTLE MAKES AN IDEAL CRACKING TOOL

OTHER USEFUL METHODS— A COFFEE MILL

JUICE EXTRACTOR OR FOOD MIXER

OR A ROLLING PIN

MASHING

The malt has now to be mashed to convert its starch to maltose, or sugar, and to extract it. Mashing is normally done in a vessel or boiler fitted with a tap, so that the wort can be drawn off, and it helps if the mash is contained in an inner vessel with a perforated bottom, standing on ½ inch oaken blocks, which will act as a strainer. Or, if you can protect the exit hole of the tap from blockage, the boiler alone can be used, and the wort be allowed to dribble from the tap.

Ideally, one needs a long mashing period, as much as eight hours, to obtain the fullest conversion and extraction, but many home brewers content themselves with a two-hour mashing, since it is in the first two hours that the major enzymatic activity occurs.

Mashing is the central and most important single process in brewing, and both the consistency of the mash and temperature control are vital if optimum conversion of starch and extraction are to be achieved.

The temperature of the mash should be between 145° F (62° C.) and 155° F. (68° C.) and should never be allowed to rise above the latter figure. The best rule of thumb is to aim at an average of 150° F., within one or two degrees, and to go as high as 153° F. for light ales and bitter, or as low as 146° F. for milds and browns. Temperature control is tricky, but can be achieved without too much difficulty, as will be seen.

If you are adopting the orthodox "mashing and sparging" method on no account use more than one gallon of liquor to $1\frac{1}{2}$ lb. malt for the two purposes combined, or you will extract more starch than you can convert and finish up with a beer which has a starch haze.

You will have worked out how much malt you need to use to produce the desired quantity of beer, but your initial mash needs to be a stiff one, with at least $4\frac{1}{2}$ lb. of malt to a gallon of liquor. So raise the temperature of the liquor to about 165° F. and use enough of it to make up a mash of this consistency. Save the remaining liquor for adding later and for sparging.

Stir in the malt and the temperature of the mash will fall slightly to about the right level—around 155° F. Thereafter aim to keep it at about 150° F., within one or two degrees, for the next half hour.

Small quantities of hot (180°–195° F.) liquor can be added after this period to maintain the heat. Stir the mash when doing so. Keep a close eye on the temperature and if necessary adjust the heat.

IODINE TEST

The optimum conversion is probably obtained in $2–2\frac{1}{2}$ hours. The way to test that all the starch has been converted to sugar is to use a solution of iodine (medical iodine diluted with an equal volume of water). Put a few drops of the wort into a white cup and add a drop of the iodine solution. If starch is still present the mixture will turn blue; if it does not it can be taken that conversion is complete.

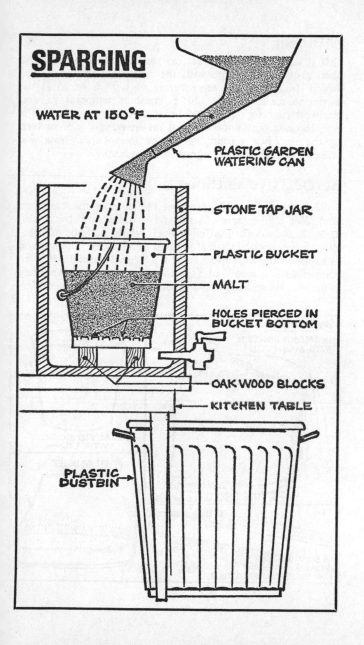

SPARGING

WATER AT 150°F

PLASTIC GARDEN WATERING CAN

STONE TAP JAR

PLASTIC BUCKET

MALT

HOLES PIERCED IN BUCKET BOTTOM

OAK WOOD BLOCKS

KITCHEN TABLE

PLASTIC DUSTBIN

SPARGING

If it is, draw off the wort, so that the mash settles, and then proceed to sparge with the remainder of the liquor, which should be at a temperature of 170° F. or so at the outset to maintain that 150° F. mashing temperature, and the wort running out should be at that temperature. If it is not, increase the temperature of the sparging liquor or turn up the heat. For sparging use a very fine watercan hose or a (clean!) garden pressure spray (see diagram).

ALTERNATIVE METHODS

Some home brewers, however (we suspect the majority) find close temperature control and sparging both tricky and tedious, and adopt short cuts which, whilst perhaps not producing immaculate results, are still satisfactory. The method is to infuse the malt in some of the liquor, maintain an even temperature by means of a thermostat, and omit the sparging process. This makes possible much longer mashing periods.

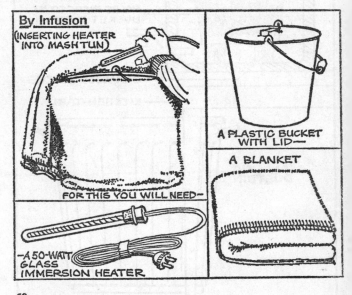

By Infusion (INSERTING HEATER INTO MASH TUN)

FOR THIS YOU WILL NEED—

—A 50-WATT GLASS IMMERSION HEATER

A PLASTIC BUCKET WITH LID—

A BLANKET

Here are two examples:

Use a 2-gallon polythene bucket or boiler, with lid. Bring just under two gallons of liquor to 65° C. (150° F.), pour them in the bucket, and scatter in 2 lb. of milled malt, or grist.

Then insert a 50-watt glass immersion heater, put the lid on the bucket, cover with a blanket or thick cloth, and leave on overnight or for a period of eight hours. The temperature with these quantities and with this type of heater will remain between 54° C. (130° F.) and 65° C. (150° F.) and extraction is first-rate. Such a heater, costing only 38p, or so, will last for years and it is quite unnecessary even to have a thermostat; current consumption is negligible.

Strain off into a boiler and make up to three, or even four, gallons. Add 2 oz. hops and 2 lb. block invert sugar. Boil for an hour. Strain, cool to 75° F., ferment, prime and bottle as usual.

An even better way is to use a Bruheat boiler, which is basically a polypropylene bucket fitted with an electric element controlled by an extremely sensitive thermostat. This is a great advantage in brewing where mashing temperatures are almost always critical in the obtaining of quality beers. The Bruheat, marketed by Ritchie products, is the simplest answer I have discovered to brewing problems.

A suitable recipe for five gallons bitter is: 7 lb. crushed pale malt, ½ lb. crushed crystal malt, 3 oz. Goldings hops, 2 lb. brewing sugar (Itona), 1 teaspoon Leigh Williams pale ale water treatment (if you live in a soft water district). Dry beer finings.

The best technique when using a Bruheat is to create a dilute mash (e.g. 7 lb. of malt to three gallons of water) and to start mashing at a low temperature and raise up to 140-145°F. range. The heating element is really good as it 'pulses' electricity for heating and allows a period of cooling in between. Consequently thermal stability (and hence a quick conversion) is achieved, and the element doesn't cause any burning of the malt sugars during the boiling processes.

The Bruheat is light and easy to handle, and the electrical system dismantles easily and safely, so a thorough cleaning can be done after every use.

BOILING

As will be seen, whichever method you use for mashing, once the process is complete the wort is ready for hopping and boiling.

The wort will usually have to be boiled at some stage mainly to extract the flavour from the hops which are added to it, to obtain the essential bitterness of beer. Use ½ oz. to 1½ oz. of hops per gallon, according to the degree of bitterness required, but hold back a small quantity to add in the last five minutes. (The aroma of the hops tends to be boiled out; this will restore it.) The wort must be boiled for at least half an hour, and preferably three-quarters, and one point to note is that boiling does darken the beer (half an hour will give a pale beer, but less will give an anaemic-looking one, and up to 1½ hours will produce a darker beer). For stouts and extra stouts, of course, black malt should be used.

FERMENTING

When the temperature has dropped to 15.5° C. (60° F.) strain off or remove the hops, give the wort a good rousing, and pitch the yeast.

Then put a cloth or blanket over the fermenting jar (or, if using a carboy, fit a fermentation lock). If 1-gallon jars are being used they can be fitted with fermentation locks in the usual way, but should be filled only to the shoulder, to allow for foaming. With open containers the first thick foam to be formed should be skimmed off, to assist subsequent clearing; if using closed jars which prevent skimming it will be found advisable to reduce the quantity of hops, or the beer may be too bitter, since much of the bitterness from them does seem to be concentrated in the first "head" which forms.

Keep the fermentation in a temperature of 18–23° C. (65–75° F.). Strong beers will ferment out in a week to 10 days (unlike in winemaking, a rapid, vigorous fermentation is to be desired), weaker ones in three days or so.

Bottle only when S.G. is between 1005 & 1010.

BOTTLING

To get the best results with home brew and certainly to produce a beer with a good head and sparkle, it is essential to use a final container which is gas-tight, and which will withstand a reasonably high pressure.

Quart beer or cider flagons are preferable. Screw-stoppered ones are ideal, since the stoppers can be used over and again, but those are now rarely obtainable, crown caps having come into general use. These can be purchased cheaply and are easily applied using a "knock on" or lever crimping tool. Make sure the bottles are sound, not cracked or chipped about the base or neck (and consequently weakened) and that any rubber washers on the stoppers or seals in the caps are are in good condition, or they will leak and the beer will be flat since pressure will be lost.

These flagons have several advantages: a quart is just enough for a sociable quick drink for two (or a long drink for one!), the beer will pour well, look well, and have that so-desirable sparkle—which also renders it slightly more potent. Beer in bottles, too, will clear more quickly than that in tap jars or pressure barrels, since the yeast has a shorter distance to fall. The only disadvantage of bottles, as compared with using a pressure barrel, is that there are 20 or so bottles to be cleaned and sterilised instead of one big vessel, but if they are in regular use for the same purpose this is not likely to be a serious drawback.

If you decide to use a 4-gallon tap-jar or pressure barrel, or a 7-pint pipkin for your beer, you have the advantage that you can draw as little as half a pint at a time, and if it is very strong that is an advantage. But in this case all the gas is usually spent immediately in forming the head, so that the beer is "draught" in character.

This can nowadays be easily overcome by using one of the modern CO_2 injectors, perhaps in combination with a neat dispenser.

Most brewers seem to prefer the convenient flagon. If you do not wish to consume the whole quart at one go, it is perfectly possible to keep a half or quarter bottle for some days, providing the stopper is screwed down again immediately, and to avoid undue wastage it is quite a good idea to pour such quarters or "bottoms" into one flagon, nearly filling it, and then stopper it and leave it to clear in the usual way. Wastage is thus reduced to the minimum.

So let us assume, first, that you have collected your flagons and are ready to set about the pleasant task of bottling your first brew. To clean them prepare a stock solution of potassium metabisulphite, by dissolving ¼ lb. in a quart of hot water. Keep it handy in a stoppered flagon. Take all the stoppers out of your bottles, and set aside those with perished washers. Take off these washers. Stretch the new washers over the ends of all the stoppers. Then take each one in turn and insert a spike (say the outside prong of an old fork) between the washer and the stopper. Then, by turning the stopper round and round, the washer can be worked down to its proper place.

Next take the bottles. Rinse each under the cold tap, emptying the water out by holding upside down and swirling round with a vigorous rotary movement. This forms a whirl-pool inside, which allows the air to get in and the water to fly out. Take a jug and in it mix two ounces of your stock sulphite solution in a pint of water. Pour this sterilising mixture through a polythene funnel from one bottle to the next. From the last bottle, pour it back into the jug, and drop all the stoppers in. Next give the stoppers and each bottle a quick rinse under the tap to remove any traces of sulphite.

Keep the remains of the sulphite solution handy for sterilising the siphon before and after use. You will find the whole job is made much easier by fitting to the cold tap a length of hose-pipe equipped with a lever-spray nozzle. The bottles are now ready to fill.

SIPHONING

You want to have the suction end of the siphon just above the sediment at the bottom of the fermenting vessel. The best way to do this is to have a length of glass tube ($\frac{1}{4}$ in. bore) with a U-bend at one end, to bring the lower opening of the tube some $\frac{3}{4}$ in. above the bottom of the U. This tube, with your polythene piping fitted at the other end can be pushed straight down into the vessel till the U-bend rests on the bottom. The opening will then be sucking up the brew just above the level of the sediment. A chemist will do this bit of glasswork. Failing that, you can buy a good adjustable siphon ready-made.

PRIMING

Put the empty bottles in their crates, and "prime" each one with one level teaspoonful of castor sugar. Use a funnel to get it down the neck cleanly, and tap the stem of the funnel each time, to make sure the whole dose goes down

This priming sugar starts a further slight fermentation, enough to give the mature drink a good sparkle. If more sugar than this is put in, you may lose the beer in foam, or burst the bottle.

The same is true if you bottle it before the fermentation in the first place has finished. Fill each in turn with the siphon, up to just beyond the shoulder. The minimum space

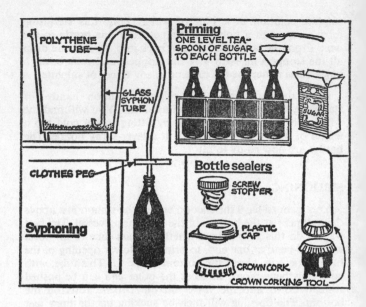

POLYTHENE TUBE

GLASS SYPHON TUBE

CLOTHES PEG

Syphoning

Priming
ONE LEVEL TEA-SPOON OF SUGAR TO EACH BOTTLE

Bottle sealers

SCREW STOPPER

PLASTIC CAP

CROWN CORK

CROWN CORKING TOOL

to leave below the stopper is one inch or you may have trouble with foam when you come to unscrew the stopper. When all are filled, screw down the stoppers. Wet the stoppers to allow the washers to slip when you tighten them, screw down hard, and give each bottle a good shake to dissolve the sugar. Store upright in a cool dark place; an appreciable drop in temperature will greatly assist in the clearing of the beer.

Subsequently, if you think it worth the trouble, the bottles can be inverted and left standing to allow the yeast to settle on the stoppers. Then, working over a sink, and preferably with the neck of the bottle held under water, the stopper can be loosened, and the yeast sediment will be blown out by the pressure, the stopper being quickly rescrewed home.

But this is really needless effort, for sediment in beer causes little waste, unless the drink is carelessly poured.

PRIMING TAP-JARS OR BARRELS

It is advisable to leave, say, a half-gallon space in a 4½- or 5-gallon pressure barrel or tap jar and put any surplus brew in bottles. The space left gives room for the gas pressure to build up. Otherwise, you risk blowing out the tap, or bursting the jar. Often a barrel may have a high pressure resistance, but the tap or taphole seal is much weaker.

To prime, make a syrup by dissolving 2 lb. of castor sugar in one pint of boiling water. Allow to cool and keep stoppered up in a sterilised flagon. For a 4-gallon jar, take 3 oz. of this syrup and add to the brew in the jar while you are siphoning. This makes enough gas to drive about half the contents out under pressure. You may experiment with more, but it hardly worth the risk, and with heavy beers it is as well to reduce the priming sugar to 1-1½ lb. to the pint, or you may even have a jar burst. It will depend on the strength of the barrel or jar; we cannot hold ourselves responsible!

Modern pressure barrels made in synthetics are now quite satisfactory, and have clean, on-off polyvinyl taps which usually give no trouble. Both these and the 7-pint pipkins can be fitted with CO_2 injectors to maintain the pressure as the beer is dispensed.

Tap jars are a little trickier. Once the jar is filled and primed, wet the rubber washer of the stopper, and screw down tight. The washer should be seen to flatten and bulge. See that the tap is hammered well home. When the gas pressure builds up the tap may leak a little. This usually stops after a few days as the corks take up the moisture and swell. If they go on leaking, the only cure is to change them. The cork shive is often hard to fit over the stem of a new tap. Soak it, but not the tap, overnight in your sterilising solution. It should then be soft enough to coax up to the shoulder of the tap, where it must be before you try to drive the tap home. If it will not go, then rasp off a little of the taper round the shoulder of the tap. There is plenty of wood to spare at that point.

If the tap grows mould, and it is almost bound to, wash it off with a strong sulphite solution.

When the pressure fails, and no more beer can be drawn off, unscrew the stopper, reprime, and wait for the brew to clear. If you have only a gallon or less left in, better draw it off into pint bottles, and prime as usual. When the tap jar is empty, clean out with water, swill it around with sulphite solution, and refill, either with your next brew or with water. If left empty, the tap and corks will dry out and become unusable.

FINING

Some authorities recommend that home brew should be fined, as commercial beer is, but I have never found this necessary, for beers stored in a cool place for a fortnight or three weeks have always cleared successfully, and indeed been brilliant.

If, however, you wish to fine your beer, it can be done quite simply by using gelatine. There are many gelatines, varying in fining power, but a good one to use is Cox's, from Boots the Chemists. A 5p box has three packets, each of which will fine two to three gallons. All that one has to do is to rack the beer, towards the end of the fermentation, into 1-gallon jars or other suitable containers, distribute the gelatine equally between them, fit air locks, and allow to stand for a week.

Then siphon into your stone jar or screw-stopper flagons and prime with sugar as usual. Leave at least a week before drinking. All winemaking supplies firms market their own finings, too.

Most beers are better if kept at least three weeks before drinking; strong beers longer.

The recipes which follow will make the procedure clear and give you an idea of the many possible variations.

LAGER
(4 gallons)

Ingredients:

4 lb. pale malt (cracked)	Lager yeast
2½ oz. Hallertauer hops	½ teaspoon citric acid
3 lb. sugar	4 gallons water (soft)

Method:

Measure out four gallons of water. Bring two gallons to 150° F. Put the malt into a 2-gallon polythene bucket and pour on to it as much of the water as possible (you will not be able to use the whole two gallons unless your bucket is slightly over-size, but this does not matter).

Insert 50-watt immersion heater, cover and wrap bucket with blanket or similar material to conserve heat, and switch on. Leave heater on for eight hours (consumption is negligible); it will hold these quantities at desired temperature (approximately 150° F.) Then strain the wort into a boiler, add 2 oz. hops, the salt, and the remaining water, bring to boil, and simmer for 40 minutes. Add a few loose hops ($\frac{1}{2}$ oz. or so). Simmer for five minutes.

Put the sugar and the citric acid into a 5-gallon polythene dustbin and strain on to them the wort. Add the balance of the water, cold, and stir thoroughly until all sugar is dissolved. Cool to 75° F., then add yeast and nutrient.

Lager yeast is a bottom fermenter, i.e. it will eventually settle well. The first head of froth which forms on the brew after two days should be skimmed off. Fermentation will normally take a week in a warm place. Keep the container well covered. Bottle when S.G. is about 1005 and certainly not above 1010, or when surface of brew clears but tiny bubbles are visible in a ring in the middle. Add one level teaspoon sugar to each quart flagon, fill to within $\frac{1}{4}$ in. of stopper, and screw down well. Store upright in cool place.

LIGHT ALE (1)
(4 gallons)

Ingredients:

1 lb. crystal malt (crushed)	2 oz. Goldings hops
1 lb. DMS malt extract	2 lb. invert sugar
1 lb. Brumore	4 gallons water (hard)
4 Vinotex Ale yeast tablets	

Method:

Heat $1\frac{1}{2}$ gallons of liquor to 148° to 150° F., add the first three items, stir well, and hold the temperature for two hours. Stir occasionally. Add hops, bring to boil, and boil gently for 30 minutes. Strain off the wort and sparge the spent grain with four pints hot water. Stir in the invert sugar and make up to four gallons with cold tap water. Pitch yeast, ferment, rack, prime and bottle as usual.

LIGHT ALE (2)
(4 gallons)

This is an excellent light ale, easily made, with the minimum of fuss and bother; the recipe ignores the finer points of brewing and involves no tricky mashing or extraction, but it does produce a palatable and pleasing light ale.

Ingredients:

1½ lb. pale malt	3 oz. Golding hops
1¾ lb. brown malt	4 gallons water (hard)
1½ lb. cracked barley	2 teaspoons brewing yeast
1½ lb. brown sugar	

Method:

The barley must be cracked with a rolling pin or coffee mill. Boil up the malt, barley and hops for 35 minutes, adding a few hops in the last five minutes, then strain on to sugar. Allow temperature to drop to 70° F., then add your yeast, a good beer or lager yeast preferably.Stand in a warm place (about 70° F.) and ferment for 48–72 hours, until the gravity has dropped to 10 or below. This will be when the surface of the beer has cleared but tiny bubbles are still rising in the centre. This light beer does not need priming; rack it straight into the bottles and the fermentation will finish in bottle, giving a clear, sparkling, fairly dry light ale. It pays to keep this beer a fortnight before drinking, although it can be "tapped" after a week!

ECONOMY PALE ALE
(2¼ gallons)

Ingredients:

½ lb. crushed maize or	2¼ gallons water
ground rice	Yeast
1¾ lb. malt	1½ oz. Golding hops

Method:

Make your main mash by steeping 1½ lb. cracked malt in half a gallon of water at 101° F. (38° C.) for quarter of an hour and keep at 86° F. (30° C.) for a further hour. Meanwhile crack ½–1 lb. of maize (or rice) and ¼ lb. malt with a rolling pin or mincer, put into half a gallon of water and bring up to 113° F. (45° C.). Hold at this temperature for half an hour, then boil for a further quarter of an hour. Mix your two mashes. Raise the temperature to 160° F. (72° C.) for the starch to sugar conversion to proceed, and when this is complete, as shown by an iodine test (page 58) heat the brew to 167° F. (75° C.) to stabilise it. The solids should then be allowed to settle and the clear wort is then run off and made up to 2½ gallons with more water. Add 2 oz. hops, a teaspoon of salt, bring to the boil, and simmer for two hours. Cool to 70° F., pitch the yeast, ferment and bottle in screw-stopper quart flagons when the gravity has dropped to 10. Leave 1¼ in. space below the stopper and add one level teaspoon of sugar to each flagon before screwing down the stopper hard. Store in a cool place for a fortnight before drinking.

STRONG PALE ALE
(4 gallons)

Ingredients:

4 lb. malt	4 gallons water (hard)
6 lb. sugar	Brewer's yeast
4 oz. Golding hops	

Method:

Crack the malt.

Measure out four gallons of water and bring two gallons of it to 150° F. Put the malt into 2-gallon polythene bucket and pour on to it as much water as possible. Insert 50-watt immersion heater, cover and wrap bucket with blanket, and switch on. Leave heater on for eight hours, keeping the temperature of the liquor at between 145° and 155° F.-Then strain the wort into a boiler, add 3 oz. hops, and the salt, bring to the boil, and simmer for 40 minutes. Add another 1 oz. hops and simmer for further five minutes.

Put the sugar into a polythene dustbin and strain on to it the wort through a nylon sieve. Stir well, bring the quantity up to four gallons with cold water, and stir thoroughly to make sure all sugar is dissolved. Allow to cool to 70° F., then cream your yeast in a pudding basin half filled with the wort, and pour this barm back into the brew. Cover closely and leave in a warm place for eight to ten days. Skim off the first foamy head which forms. Afterwards (if using a top fermenting yeast) the yeast will form a dirty brown "pancake" on the surface of the brew. Skim this. Subsequently the yeast will sink, though some of it may remain on the surface. Prime and bottle when the S.G. is *below* 1010 (after nine or ten days).

BEST BITTER
(4 gallons)

Ingredients:

5 lb. pale malt	12 oz. Brewing flour
8 oz. crystal malt	5 oz. Golding hops
12 oz. flaked maize	4 gallon water (hard)
12 oz. DMS malt extract	Bass Red Label yeast

Method:

The barley grain should first be cracked in a liquidiser, but be careful to only half fill with grain. (If the container is filled you will end up with a very fine flour at the bottom and whole grains at the top, which is not, of course, the even grist we aim to obtain.)

Mash the grains, flour and Malt extract for three hours at a temperature between 145° F. and 155° F., and strain and sparge the grains. Then boil the wort with the hops for 45 mins. When the wort has cooled to 60° F. take a hydrometer reading and adjust the starting gravity to 1042 with granulated sugar. Pitch with a top fermenting yeast if Red label is unobtainable and ferment at 65°-70° F. to dryness before priming and bottling. Being a high gravity beer this bitter is best kept for at least five weeks before drinking.

The quantity of hops quoted has been well tried, but it should be remembered that the quality and standard of hops is far from constant, and it may be necessary to make minor adjustments, from year to year, or even during the same year, for, towards the end of a season, hops that have been in storage for a long period of time will have deteriorated.

BRUHEAT BITTER

(5 gallons)

For this recipe you will need a Bruheat boiler, a 2-gallon enamel bucket, and a 5-gallon plastic barrel or tap-jar.

Ingredients:

7 lb. crushed pale malt	½ lb. crushed crystal malt
2 lb. brewing sugar (Itona)	3 oz. Goldings hops
1 teaspoon Pale Ale water treatment (if water is soft)	Dry beer finings (Leigh-Williams)

Method:

Bring 1½ gallons water to 170° F.—add Pale Ale water treatment—carefully pour in grain malt, mixing slowly. The temperature will have dropped to 150° F. when all the malt is mixed. Place the enamel bucket into electric oven previously set at 200° F. You will find you have a mash of about the same consistency as porridge. Leave two hours— no attention needed providing you commenced at the correct temperature. After two hours place muslin or nylon straining cloth over the dustbin—(use clothes pegs around the top of the bin to hold the cloth in place) and pour the mash over this; sparge the grains with three gallons water at 170° F. or thereabouts (previously heated to this temperature in Burco boiler).

Add 2 lb. brewing sugar to the wort and stir to dissolve. Place in boiler and add water to about 5½ gallons. Add hops, retaining a handful or so and boil for two hours, this two hour boil is needed to enable the insolubles to coagulate for crystal clear beer. Add retained hops about 15 minutes befor completion.

Strain into plastic dustbin and cool to 70° F., add top fermenting yeast. One cultured from Guinness does the job admirably. Fermentation usually takes about three days and finishes at gravity 10. Skim off thick pad of yeast and retain some of the cleanest for future brews. Siphon into barrel and add 20 teaspoons sugar and finings, previously prepared·

Leave seven days, when it will be ready to consume. If anyone wishes to bottle this beer the procedure would be to siphon into bottles and add ½ teaspoon of sugar per pint, but it then takes about two to three weeks to mature.

BIRMINGHAM ALE
(4 gallons)

Ingredients:

4 lb. pale malt (crushed)	2 lb. crystal malt (cracked)
3 oz. Goldings hops	1½ lb. brewing sugar
4 gal. water (Birmingham's is said to be excellent for this brew)	Yeast: cultured from 2 bottles of Guinness

Method:

Bring about six pints water to 170° F. and pour into warmed enamel bucket, add the grain and test temperature, if this has dropped below 150° F. raise to this figure with hot water until temperature is uniform throughout the mash. Place in gas oven (all shelves removed) on Regulo mark "low", leave to mash for two hours. Great care is required in this mashing to avoid temperatures more or less than 150° F. as this is the most critical part of the whole operation. If the mashing should fail then insufficient extraction would be the result—disastrous.

Now strain into boiler, add water to four gallons and the brewing sugar and the hops, but keep back about ½ oz. of the latter until later.

Boil for two hours then add the ½ oz. of hops and simmer for five minutes.

Strain into fermenting bin and leave to cool to 70° F.

Take S.G. This should be about 40–45° which will give a potential alcoholic content of 4½% which is about right for this type of brew

Pitch yeast and ferment down to 10° before barrelling (about three days). Prime with 16 level teaspoonsful of castor sugar and add about one-third of a pint of Leigh-Williams

Beer Finings made to the maker's instructions. Wait a week or ten days—then "Good Health!"

BITTER
(4 gallons)

Ingredients:

2 lb. crystal malt
2 lb. tin Golden Syrup
Beer yeast

2 lb. pale malt
3 oz. Golding hops
4 gallons water (hard)

Method:

Bring the water in the boiler up to 150° F. Add the cracked malt and maintain at a temperature of 140°-150° F. for four hours. It is most important that the temperature never exceeds 150° F. Strain off the wort. Add the hops and salt and boil for an hour. Strain again and add the syrup. Allow to cool to 65° F. and add the yeast. Ferment at between 65° and 70° F. for four days. To a large 1-gallon pressure barrel add two tablespoons of sugar, and then siphon in your home brew. All sediment will sink under the level of the tap, if you are using the usual home-brew type of barrel. Leave in the barrel, which must be quite airtight, for a week to ten days. Your home-brew is then ready to drink, and should prove a really satisfying and nourishing drink. To make a stout-like drink reduce the hops to 2 oz. and include 1 lb. of black malt and 2 lb. of crushed barley in place of the crystal malt.

MILD ALE

Ingredients:

4 lb. crystal malt (cracked)
1 lb. flaked maize
4 lb. dark brown sugar
4 gallons water (soft)
1 dessertspoonful caramel

4 oz. hops
Yeast and nutrient
1 teaspoon each salt and
   citric acid

Method:

The ale is best made by those living in a soft water district Crack the malt.

Measure out four gallons of water, and bring two gallons of it to 150° F. Put the malt and flaked maize into 2-gallon polythene bucket and pour on to it as much water as possible. Insert 50-watt immersion heater, cover and wrap bucket with blanket, and switch on. Leave heater on for eight hours, keeping the temperature of the liquor at between 145° and 155° F. Then strain the wort into a boiler, add 3½ oz. hops, and the salt, bring to the boil, and simmer for 40 minutes. Add another ½ oz. hops and the caramel (Crosse & Blackwell's liquid gravy browning) and simmer for further five minutes.

Put the sugar into a polythene dustbin, with the citric acid, and strain on to it the wort through a nylon sieve. Stir well, bring the quantity up to four gallons with cold water, and stir thoroughly to make sure all sugar is dissolved. Allow to cool to 70° F., then cream your yeast in a pudding basin half filled with the wort, and pour this barm back into the brew. Cover closely and leave in a warm place for eight to ten days. Skim off the first foamy head which forms. Afterwards (if using a top fermenting yeast) the yeast will form a dirty brown "pancake" on the surface of the brew. Skim this. Subsequently the yeast will sink, though some of it may remain on the surface. Bottle when the S.G. is *below* 1010 (after nine or ten days). Do not bottle above this S.G.— it is better to add more water if you are impatient. Fill quart flagons with a siphon to within an inch of stopper, and add one level teaspoon of sugar to each. Screw down hard and store bottles upright in a cool place until ale clears.

BROWN ALE (1)

Ingredients:

8 oz. crystal malt (cracked)
1 lb. black malt (lightly cracked)
3 oz. Fuggles hops
4 gallons water (soft)

1 lb. Brewing flour
4 lb. DMS malt extract
1 lb. invert sugar
4 Vinotex yeast tablets

Method:

Same procedure as Light Ale (1), adding the black malt at the same time as the crystal malt. If you wish to increase the body also add, say, 8 oz. flaked barley.

BROWN ALE (2)

Ingredients:

5 lb. pale malt	2½ oz. Fuggles hops
4 lb. roasted malt	4 gallons water (softened
2 lb. brewing sugar	if necessary)
2 teaspoons salt	Brewer's yeast

Method:

Measure out your four gallons of water, put two to one side, and bring the other two up to 150° F. in a boiler. Put the malt into a 2-gallon polythene bucket and pour over it as much of the water as possible (keep the small amount left for adding with the balance of the water later). Insert 50-watt immersion heater, wrap and cover bucket with blanket to conserve heat and switch on. Leave heater on for eight hours, keeping temperature between 145° and 155° F. Then strain the liquor back into the boiler, add the hops and salt, bring to the boil and simmer for 40 minutes; add ½ oz. loose hops and simmer for further five minutes. Put the brewing sugar into a 5-gallon polythene dustbin, and strain the wort on to it through a nylon sieve. Stir well to amalgamate, then add the remaining water, cold, and stir thoroughly again. Cool to 70° F. before adding the yeast and nutrient. Dip out a little of the wort with a pudding basin or jug, and cream the brewer's yeast into it, crushing it with a spoon, then tip all the milky "barm" back into the brew. Cover closely and leave in a warm place. Skim off the head of foam after 48 hours. When the surface of the brew clears, but tiny bubbles are still visible in a ring in the centre, bottle (S.G. must be below 1010 and, preferably, about 1005). Fermentation usually takes eight to ten days.

Fill quart flagons to within an inch of stopper, add one level teaspoon of sugar to each, and screw down hard. The ale will clear in about a fortnight if kept in a cool place.

BARLEY WINE
(1 gallon)
by P. Bryant

True "barley wine" can only be made successfully by using malted barley as the main ingredient. Malt extract will never give the full, malty flavour required, whatever quantity is used. Therefore, the amateur's first problem is to obtain a good sample of pale malt barley which can be used in quantity without imparting a harsh flavour to the brew.

The best adjunct to use is flaked rice or polished barley, which help to provide body. I have tried flaked maize, corn-flakes, ground rice, oat flakes and dried bananas, but for this recipe prefer one of the two above-mentioned adjuncts.

Ingredients:

1¾ lb. pale malted barley	1 level teaspoon ammonium
2 oz. flaked rice or 4 oz.	sulphate
polished barley	1 level teaspoon gypsum
1 oz. hops	½ teaspoon salt
1 lb. sugar	1 Campden tablet
1 level teaspoon citric acid	Grey Owl champagne yeast
1 gallon water	

Method:

Pick over and then put malted barley and adjunct through mincer to form the grist.

Heat one gallon of water to 68° C. in 12-pint saucepan on very low gas; add grist and maintain temperature at 62 68° C. for two hours.

Strain through kitchen sieve and then replace wort in saucepan, add hops and gypsum and boil for 40 minutes. Strain again, cool and take S.G., which should be around 48.

Add 1 lb. sugar, Campden tablet, citric acid, ammonium sulphate, salt and Grey Owl champagne yeast, and commence fermenting in a 2-gallon polythene bucket with lid. Fermentation will be strong within 12 hours. Skim brown scum from surface each day and after two days siphon into gallon jar and fit fermentation lock. When clearing begins (which may be after six weeks) rack and refit lock. When clear, rack again, cork up and store for six months, after which it may be bottled.

ANDOVER STOUT

Ingredients:

4 lb. pale malt (crushed)	2½ oz. Fuggles hops
2 lb. patent black malt	2 teaspoons salt
2 lb. crystal malt	½ teaspoon citric acid
2 lb. brewing sugar, or	Brewer's yeast
Golden Syrup	4 gallons water (softened)

Method:

Culture your own Guinness or stout yeast as explained on page 39. Failing this, buy a good quality beer yeast.

Bring two gallons of water up to 150° F. in a boiler. Pour most of this into a 2-gallon polythene bucket, and then sprinkle in the three different sorts of malt (the black malt gives your stout the desired dark colouring and woody tang). Insert your 50-watt immersion heater and switch on; cover bucket closely with blanket and wrap it to conserve heat. Keep the heater on for eight hours, holding the temperature at between 145° F. and 155° F. Then strain the wort back into the boiler, add 2 oz. hops and the salt, bring to the boil and simmer for 40 minutes. Add the remaining ½ oz. hops and simmer for five minutes. Put the 2 lb. golden syrup and the citric acid into a polythene dustbin and strain the wort on to them. Stir thoroughly, bring the total volume up to four gallons by adding the remainder of the water, cold, and stir again.

When cool, add the yeast starter and stand container, closely covered, in a warm place. The fermentation will be going well after 48 hours; skim on the third day. Ferment for about ten days until gravity drops below 1010, or surface of brew clears around the edges of the circle. Bottle in quart flagons by means of a siphon, filling to within an inch of stopper, after adding one level teaspoonful of sugar to each, Screw down stoppers hard, and store bottles upright in a cool place until stout has cleared.

BIRMINGHAM STOUT

Ingredients:

4 lb. pale malt (crushed)
1 lb. roasted (or black) malt
1½ lb. brewing sugar
3 oz. hops
Yeast (culture from two
bottles of Guinness, see
page 39)

1 lb. crystal malt
1 lb. flaked barley
1 level teaspoon salt
4 gallons water

Method:

As for Birmingham Ale (page 74).

MILK STOUT

Ingredients:

2 lb. patent black malt
6 oz. flaked barley
2 lb. glucose (powdered)
4 gallons of water (soft)

4 lb. pale malt (crushed)
Brewing yeast
2 oz. hops
1 teaspoon salt

Method:

Culture a stout or Guinness yeast (see page 39). Failing this, buy a good quality beer yeast.

Bring two gallons of water up to 150° F., in a boiler. Pour most of this into a 2-gallon polythene bucket, and then sprinkle in the pale malt, the black malt, and the 6 oz. of flaked barley (the black malt gives your stout the desired dark colouring and woody tang, while the barley, or grit, provides extra strength economically). Insert your 50-watt immersion heater and switch on, cover bucket closely with blanket and wrap it to conserve heat. Keep the heater on for eight hours, holding the temperature at between 145° F. and 155° F. Then strain the wort back into the boiler, add 1½ oz. of hops and the salt, bring to the boil and simmer for 40 minutes. Add the remaining ½ oz. of hops and simmer for five minutes. Put the 2 lb. powdered glucose into a polythene dustbin and strain the wort on to them. Stir thoroughly, bring the total volume up to four gallons by adding the remainder of the water, cold, and stir again.

When cool, add the yeast starter and stand container, closely covered, in a warm place. The fermentation will be going well after 48 hours; skim on the third day. Ferment

for about ten days until gravity drops below 1010, or surface
of brew clears around the edges of the circle. Bottle in quart
flagons by means of a siphon, filling to within an inch of
stopper, after adding one level teaspoonful of sugar to each.

OATMEAL STOUT (1)

Ingredients:

¾ lb. rye	6 oz. oatmeal
½ lb. black malt	2 oz. hops
½ lb. pale malt	4 lb. sugar
2 teaspoons brewing yeast	½ teaspoon citric acid
and nutrient	4 gallons water (soft)

Method:

Bring two gallons of water up to 150° F. in a boiler.
Pour most of this into a polythene 2-gallon bucket, and then
sprinkle in the malts, rye and oatmeal. Insert your 50-watt
immersion heater and switch on; cover bucket closely with
blanket and wrap it to conserve heat. Keep the heater on
for eight hours, holding the temperature at between 145° F.
and 155° F. Then strain the wort back into the boiler, add
1½ oz. of hops and the salt, bring to the boil and simmer for
40 minutes. Add the remaining ½ oz. of hops and simmer for
five minutes. Put the 4 lb. sugar and the citric acid into a
polythene dustbin and strain the wort on to them. Stir
thoroughly, bring the total volume up to four gallons by
adding the remainder of the water, cold, and stir again.

When cool, add the yeast starter and stand container,
closely covered, in a warm place. The fermentation will be
going well after 48 hours; skim on the third day. Ferment
for about ten days until gravity drops below 1010, or surface
of brew clears around the edges of the circle. Bottle in quart
flagons by means of a siphon, filling to within an inch of
stopper, after adding one level teaspoonful of sugar to each.

OATMEAL STOUT (another version)

A variation, using the same method:

Ingredients:

2 lb. roasted malt	3 oz. hops
2 lb. crystal malt	Yeast and nutrient
4 lb. dark brown sugar	½ teaspoon citric acid
1 lb. flaked maize	4 gallons water (soft)

Using kits or malt extract

Many people are first attracted to home brewing by one of the wide range of beer kits which are now available, and which make the production of ample supplies of beer really easy. There are kits for bitter, pale ale, stout, lager, brown ale—the lot!

Quality tends to vary according to price, as one would expect, but there is no denying that the leading kits give one beers that are every bit as good as commercial brands, and often both better and stronger, as an independent survey by "Which" in 1972 revealed. They declared that the kits which produced the most *consistently* drinkable results were Boots, Carters, Cumbria, Karswood, Tom Caxton and Unican. These were also the beers which came top for taste. Of these Boots, Tom Caxton and Unican were easier to make, and Boots was reckoned to be the "best buy."

Most kits are very simple to use, some of them involving little more than adding water and yeast so that home brewing becomes delightfully simple, and merely a matter of following that particular kit's instructions. This is what many people want, and they will always prefer kits, but naturally one has to pay for this sophistication, and you may be casting about for a cheaper, but still convenient, method.

If so, it will pay you to buy simply a good proprietary malt extract, usually sold in 1lb. or 2 lb. jars or in 14 lb. packs. Avoid, for fairly obvious reasons, "Malt and Cod Liver Oil!"

The occasionally "nutty" flavour malt extract can be minimised by using 1 lb. of unmalted whole barley for each four gallons you are making. Soak the barley in water for two or three days, pressure cook for 30 minutes in three pints of water (or boil till grains split) and then boil this barley mash with the hops when you are extracting their flavour.

When using malt extract the usual method is to infuse the hops in the boiling water, or in some of the water, and then strain the hopped liquid on to the malt extract (and sugar, if used). Any remaining water is then added, cold, and when the wort has cooled the yeast is pitched.

If one wishes to economise, household sugar can be substituted for some of the malt, and one can thus obtain varying strengths of flavour and varying alcoholic strengths. A good rule of thumb is that 1½–2 lb. per gallon will give an exceedingly strong beer, and about 1 lb. per gallon will produce weaker beers. So all one needs to remember is that the amount of "sugar" (i.e. the combined weight of malt extract and sugar) can range anywhere between 1 lb. and 2 lb. to the gallon.

Many people start out by making the strongest possible beers, but eventually they are usually content to settle for medium-strength ones, which have less disastrous after-effects and can be drunk in the quantity that a beer drinker prefers. Strong beers will ferment out in a week to ten days, weaker ones in three or four days.

If your local water is *soft*, you will probably succeed best with milds, browns and stouts, but if you wish to make a good pale ale or bitter it will help if you add one teaspoon of plaster of paris per gallon of water. If your local water is *hard*, you will do best to make bitter or pale ale, and will find it an advantage to boil *all* the water rather than to use the cold brew method. The addition of a little salt also helps.

From the recipe table overleaf, which was devised a few years ago by Mr. Humfrey Wakefield and since used successfully by thousands of brewers all over the world, you can compile your own recipes to obtain exactly the brew you require.

Those who want a light beer for summer drinking in quantity will prefer No. 1, those who want an "ordinary" bitter strength will choose No. 2. those who want "best bitter" strength No. 3, and those who want really strong beer of "barley wine" strength No. 4. The stronger the beer, the less it can be drunk in quantity and, of course, the more expensive it is to make. Most home brewers will come to prefer the strengths of Nos. 2 and 3.

To make Five Gallons

Recipe			1	2	3	4
Alcohol	..	..	3%	5%	7%	9%
Gravity at Start	..		30	45	60	80
Gravity at Finish	..		–2	0	5	9
Gallons Water			5	5	5	5
1 lb. sugar	..	..	3	4	5	6
1 lb. Malt Extract	..		1	2	3	4
Hops ..	..	..	1½ oz.	2 oz.	4–6 oz.	6–8 oz.
Price per pint	..		1p	1½p	2p	2½p
Days to clear..	..		7	14	21	28
Keeps for	..	..	Weeks	Months	Months	Years

Use also in each case: 1 pkt. Dried Yeast,
1 pkt. Yeast Food,
2 teaspoon salt, or water treatment as instructed.
Juice of one lemon.

For Stout: Boil up ½ lb. patent black malt grains and 4 oz. flaked barley with the hops, in Recipe 3 or 4.

THE PROCEDURE

Malt extract, as already pointed out, is the easiest ingredient to use because excellent results can be obtained from a "cold brew", i.e. one where it is unnecessary to boil the whole of the wort. Some experienced brewers, however, *do* prefer to boil the whole wort to ensure its complete sterility, and if you have a large enough boiler there is no reason why all the ingredients should not be put in it and boiled together.

Otherwise bring to the boil as much water as your boiler will take, say two or three gallons (after room has been left for the hops and the vigour of the boiling). Add the hops, salt or water treatment, and caramel colouring. Simmer for 45 minutes; add a few extra hops in the last five minutes. Put the sugar and malt extract into the fermenting vessel; the malt will pour more easily if the jars are stood in hot water for ten minutes first, and any remaining in the jar can be rinsed out with hot water. Strain the near-boiling infusion on to the malt and sugar. (If using a carboy, partly fill it with cold water first, and use a plastic funnel, to avoid cracking it.) Make up with cold or warm water to the required final volume, and add citric acid. It helps to have four and five gallon marks inside your fermenting vessel. Leave enough room for the frothing which will take place. Allow to cool to 70° F. and then add yeast and nutrient.

WITH ADDED MALT AND GRITS

Remember that if you are using grain malt or other grits to support your extract, to improve the flavour and/or colour the beer you are making, you will need to follow a slightly different procedure, for in this case you will need to observe the mashing principles for grain malt beers if you are to obtain the maximum value from your grain.

In this case put the grain, the extract and any water treatment being used into about half the water, say 1½ gallons, raise temperature to 150° F , and hold it closely to this temperature for about three-quarters of an hour.

Then add the hops, boil for half an hour, and strain on to any additional sugar, before making up to the required quantity with more water. Pale and crystal malts should be cracked, heavily roasted malts used whole.

The water should be adjusted to hard or soft at the outset by means of the appropriate treatment.

FERMENTING

If possible introduce yeast (creamed in a little of the wort) at 70° F. or thereabouts. Ferment for three to seven days at a temperature of about 65° F., and keep temperature as constant as possible, or varying lengths of fermentation will result. The lower the temperature, the slower the ferment, the higher the temperature (below, say, 75) the faster the ferment. A consistent temperature is more important than a high one, so keep the fermentation vessel away from draughts, and cover with blanket if necessary. If room temperature is low, use a small immersion heater coupled to a thermostat. Check occasionally with a thermometer, and do not let temperature exceed 80° F., or yeast may be killed.

If using an open crock or polythene dustbin, cover with a thick cloth or blanket, and rest the lid on top. If using a carboy, fit a fermentation lock. The first "head" of froth which forms on the brew evidently carries up with it much of the aromatic oils of the hops, for if you taste it you will see that it has a pronounced bitterness that lingers unpleasantly in the back of the throat, and your beer may later have this quality, a stronger bitterness than the one we seek, and tasted further back in the throat. So skim it off. If you are reluctant to throw away the skimmed foam (and it does seem a shame) leave it on the brew, but in that case cut down drastically on the hops.

If, despite your precautions, you eventually produce a beer which is too bitter for your taste, the bitterness can be masked by the use of liquorice. Dissolve a 3p stick in a saucepan over the stove, with a little hot water, and add the resulting syrup to your brew "to taste", that is, a little at a time, until it seems to you that it has done the trick.

With a "closed" fermentation and a "bottom" yeast (one which works from the bottom) further skimming is unnecessary. After the initial frothing and the formation of the exciting "corona", or ring, the "head" may turn a dirty brown. Do not worry about this; all is in order.

With strong beers, add half the sugar at the outset, the remainder after three days, stirring thoroughly; if all the sugar is used at the outset they may "stick" at 1020 or so.

When the surface of the beer begins to clear, but bubbles collect in a ring in the centre (or when the S.G. is below 1010, and as near as possible to 1000) you can bottle.

Priming—for Head and Sparkle

If your beer is put straight into bottles or tap jars at this stage, it will have little of that so-desirable head and sparkle, and will be "draught" in character. To obtain the sparkle it is necessary to add 1 level teaspoonful of sugar to each quart beer-bottle, which is enough to start a slight fermentation in the bottle, and give the drink a good sparkle. **DO NOT EXCEED THIS QUANTITY**, or you will have a burst bottle or, when the stopper is unscrewed, a Vesuvius of foam.

Use a funnel and prime each bottle with one level teaspoon of castor sugar, then fill to within 1¼ in. of bottom of stopper. Wet the stoppers and screw down hard. Keep the bottles in a reasonably warm place (about 65° F.) for two days, then move into a cooler one, such as the larder, to assist clarification.

(Four Gallons)
For procedures see page 84

LIGHT LAGER (1)

3½ lb. malt extract
2 oz. Hallertauer hops
Lager yeast

4 gallons water (soft)
½ teaspoon citric acid

★
LAGER (2)

5 lb. malt extract (DMS)
4 lb. pale malt
4 lb. sugar

4 oz. Saaz hops
4 gallons water (soft)
Lager yeast

★
LIGHT ALE (1)

6 lb. malt extract
2 lb. barley
1 dessertspoon caramel
3 oz. Hallertauer hops

4 gallons water (hard)
½ teaspoon citric acid
Lager yeast

★
LIGHT ALE (2)

5 lb. malt extract (DMS)
2 lb. pale malt
1 lb. flaked barley
1 lb. brewing sugar

4 oz. Golding hops
4 gallons water (hard)
Beer yeast

★
BITTER (1)

2 lb. malt extract
2 lb. white sugar
3 oz. Boots hops
1 dessertspoon caramel colouring

4 gallons water (hard)
½ teaspoon of citric acid
2 teaspoons dried beer yeast

BITTER (2)

4 lb. C.A. malt extract
8 dessertspoons medium dark
  dried malt extract
4 oz. hops

1½ lb. granulated sugar
4 gallons water (hard)
Brewing yeast

BITTER (3)

6 lb. malt extract
3 lb. pale malt
3 lb. sugar

6 oz. Golding hops
4 gallons water (hard)
Brewer's yeast

★

BERRY BREW
(Best Bitter)

4 lb. malt extract
4 lb. sugar
1 level teaspoon citric acid
2 level teaspoons salt
4-5 gallons water

4 oz. hops
1 dessertspoonful caramel
(Crosse & Blackwells
    gravy browning) boiled
    with hops
Brewers' yeast

★

MILD (draught)

4 lb. C.A. malt extract
2 lb. crystal malt
4 gallons water (soft)
Brewer's yeast

1 lb. pale malt
1½ lb. glucose chippings
4 oz. Fuggles hops

★

BROWN ALE (1)

4 lb. C.A. malt extract
1½ lb. medium dark dried
    malt extract
½ lb. sugar
4 gallons water (soft)
Beer yeast

½ lb. black malt
½ oz. crystal malt
1⅛ oz. Fuggles hops
1 lb. lactose (dissolved in
    ½ pint boiling water and
    added before bottling)

★

BROWN ALE (2)

2 lb. malt extract
4 lb. brown sugar
8 oz. black malt
1½ oz. Fuggles hops

½ teaspoon salt
4 gallons water (soft)
Brewer's yeast

★

SWEET BROWN ALE

2 lb. malt extract
4 lb dark sugar
2 oz. hops
2 teaspoons yeast

16 oz. lactose
Water to 4 gallons (soft)
8 oz. black malt grains

N.B.—The lactose is dissolved in half a pint of boiling water, cooled, and added to the ale before bottling (i.e. 1 oz. to each quart flagon.

★
DARK BROWN ALE

2 lb. malt extract	4 lb. brown sugar
2 oz. hops	Water to 4 gallons (soft)
4 sticks liquorice boiled	Stout yeast

★
STRONG BROWN ALE

½ lb. milled black malt	½ teaspoon citric acid
3½ lb. malt extract	Water to 4 gallons (soft)
4 lb. brown sugar	Brewers' yeast
4 oz. Fuggles hops	

★
PORTER

2 lb. malt extract	4 gallons water (soft)
1 lb. patent black malt	3 oz. Fuggles hops
1 lb. flaked barley	Brewers' yeast
2 lb. white sugar	

★
STOUT

2 lb. malt extract	1 teaspoon salt
½ lb. pale malt	boiled with 3 oz. hops for
1 lb. patent black malt	30 mins.
3 lb. dark brown sugar	Water to 4 gallons (soft)
	Stout yeast

★
OATMEAL STOUT

6 lb. malt extract	8 oz. lactose
1 lb. black malt	6 oz. Fuggles hops
2 lb. oatmeal	4 gallons water (soft)
4 lb. sugar	Cultured stout yeast

Dissolve lactose in half pint of boiling water, cool, and add before bottling.

★
DOUBLE STOUT (Good for you!)

5½ lb. DMS malt extract	2 level teaspoons salt
1 lb. black malt, cracked	4½ gallons water (soft)
12 oz. flaked barley	4 oz. Fuggles hops
	Cultured stout yeast

VINEBREW
By F. E. Lee, Lee-on-Solent

Ingredients:

2 lb. malt extract
3 lb. Demerara sugar
4-6 oz. hops
1 teaspoon of powdered
   gelatine

1 lb. black treacle (or
   Golden Syrup)
2 oz. yeast (brewers' or
   1 packet Heath and
   Heather)
4 gallons water

Method:

The yeast should be creamed by mixing with a little sugar with a fork. It should then be kept in a warm room so that it is fully active by the time your beer is cool enough.

Put the water into the container and bring to the boil, then stir in the sugar and syrup, making sure it does not catch on the bottom and burn. Now add the hops and boil for 45 minutes. Remove the hops (if in a bag) and squeeze well. Don't burn your hand—let it cool before squeezing.

When the liquid has dropped to 160° F., stir in the malt extract then, when the temperature has further dropped to 65° F., add the yeast and stir it in well. The container should be covered now with several thicknesses of cloth to exclude air.

After an interval of 12 hours the yeast growth will be several inches thick and most of this should be skimmed off, leaving about half an inch. Skim again each day until about the fourth day the liquid is cleared at each operation. On the fourth day remove about a pint of the liquid and warm, but do not boil, add to this the gelatine powder and when completely dissolved stir into the main brew. The beer will now start to clarify. Now is the time to colour the beer by using gravy powder; a dessertspoonful will be sufficient for four gallons.

The fermentation should be complete by the sixth or seventh day and bottling should commence when nothing but few isolated flecks of foam are all that show on the surface after an interval of about eight hours has elapsed after the last skimming. The beer completely clarifies only after it has been bottled, so don't worry if it seems cloudy at the time of bottling. Before putting beer into the bottles put a saltspoon of sugar into each bottle; this will enable the small amount of yeast still in suspension to ferment sufficiently to produce enough carbonic acid gas to give the beer a good sparkle and head when poured.

The beer will be ready for drinking in ten days, but you will find a small amount of sediment in the bottom, so pour out carefully.

BIER DEWEJO

A very popular recipe by Dean Jones, of St. Anne's on Sea

1. Ingredients (for ten gallons)

   (a) 8 oz. hops.
   (b) 3 lb. malt extract.
   (c) 8 lb. granulated sugar.
   (d) 1 tablespoon caramel (solution of burnt sugar) (Boots).
   (e) 1 tablespoon Allinson's dried yeast.
   (f) 2 packets water treatment.

2. (a) Bring 7 oz. hops to the boil in about 1½ gallons of water, simmer for 20 minutes.

   (b) Strain 2 quarts of hop water on to 2 lb. malt and 2 lb. sugar. Dissolve, add cold water to cool to about 70° F.

   (c) Repeat 2(b) above, using 1 lb. malt and 2 lb. sugar.

   (d) Add 2 quarts of boiling water to hops, and 1 oz. hops. Strain off water and add to caramel and 2 lb. sugar Dissolve and cool to 70° F. by adding cold water.

   (e) Place wort in either a 10-gallon carboy or 12-gallon plastic dustbin. Add warm (70° F.) water to make up to seven gallons.

   (f) Put yeast into jug of: 6 oz. warm water, 1 teaspoon sugar and 1 teaspoon golden syrup (dissolve). Stir well, cover and keep in warm place for about ten minutes.

   (g) Add yeast and water treatment, stir and cover with two or three layers of butter muslin.

3. The Brewing

   (a) Keep brew in temperature of 75°–78° F., if possible, avoid temperatures below 55° F. and above 80° F.

91

(b) After 24 hours, dissolve the remaining 2 lb. of sugar in two gallons of warm water and add to brew.

(c) After 48 hours, add slightly sweetened warm water to make the brew up to ten gallons. Do this in stages and avoid an overflow.

4. The Bottling

(a) When all fermentation has ceased and the brew starts to clear, then you may bottle (three to four days).

(b) Use pint or quart screw-stopper bottles. (Tolly bottles are excellent.)

(c) Fill each bottle to about 1½ inches of the top, add a scant teaspoon of castor sugar, screw stopper in firmly, shake and put away.

(d) Store in a medium temperature, 50°–60° F. The beer will clear within a week, but keep it at least three weeks before drinking. This beer has been kept as long as six months and was excellent.

5. Your Reward

(a) Decant your beer into a quart jug (to allow for foam) and then fill your glasses.

(b) Should the beer be too lively and difficult to decant, cool it off in the fridge for an hour.

(c) Wash your bottles as you empty them. It saves a lot of time when you come to bottle your next brew Do NOT use detergent for washing beer glasses or bottles. It kills the "head".

Prosit!

CANADIAN LAGER

This recipe is for a lager specially suited to the Canadian palate:

Kit required:

1 six Imperial gallon primary fermentation vessel (plastic preferred),

1 five Imperial gallon plastic or glass carboy and fermentation lock,

1 five-foot siphon tube,

1 plastic sheet (1 yd. sq.) to cover primary vessel,

1 Specific Gravity of Brix hydrometer and testing jar,

1 stainless steel or enamel vessel, not less than 1 Imperial
gallon,
1 wooden or stainless steel spoon,
1 bottle capper for crown caps,
5 dozen beer bottles, tall or stubby,
1 immersion type thermometer.

Ingredients:

5 Imperial gallons of water
1 2½ lb. tin of light barley malt
extract
½ oz. Kent finishing hops
2 oz. Bramling or Cluster hops
4 lb. of corn sugar (Dextrose)
1 teaspoon citric acid
2–3 teaspoons of salt
½ teaspoon yeast energiser
½ teaspoon special beer finings
1 teaspoon heading liquid
Lager beer yeast or ale yeast

NOTE—The addition of
1 teaspoon of ascorbic
acid at time of bottling
will reduce the hazard of
oxidation.

Method:

Be sure to save two full cups of corn sugar for bottling;
then make sure your yeast starter is ready to use. Boil as
much of the water as possible. Naturally, this will depend
on the size of the container you have, but not less than one
gallon. Along with the water you should boil the malt extract,
2 ozs. of hops (broken up and tied in cheesecloth), the salt
and citric acid. Simmer very gently for 1–2 hours with a lid
on to reduce evaporation. As you remove this from the heat,
add the ½ oz. of Kent hops which can remain in the "wort"
during the primary fermentation. Pour this hot wort over the
corn sugar (minus the two cups, remember). Stir to dissolve
the sugar and add the balance of the water to make up a
total of five Imperial gallons.

Cover the "wort" with a sheet of plastic tied down and
allow the mixture to cool to around 60° F. This may take
up to 12 hours, so don't hold your breath. The fermentation
vessel should be in a place where the temperature will remain
between 55° and 65° F. When the "wort" is cool, take a
Specific Gravity reading to make sure it is between 33 and 38.

(The starting gravity should be 30 to 40, and the beer should finish at 0, i.e., 1.035 to 1.000). If it is not correct, you can adjust it by adding more sugar or water, depending on whether it is high or low.

Now add the active beer yeast and cover once again with the plastic sheet. After about four or five days of active ferment you can start checking the Specific Gravity to see how the ferment is progressing. It will probably take six to ten days to get down to between 5 to 10 (1.010) depending on the temperature. When it gets to this point, skim off the floating hops, add the yeast energiser, and siphon the wort into the carboy. Don't fill the carboy too full because you need room to add the "finings" at this point. Dissolve the half teaspoon of finings in one cup of very hot water (not boiling) and pour this on top of the beer in the carboy and stir in thoroughly with the handle end of your wooden spoon. The carboy should now be filled to within two or three inches of the fermentation lock which should be properly attached at this time.

Now that your beer is in the carboy with the fermentation lock attached and placed in a cool (55°–65° F.), place away from the light, it is safe even if you don't get to look at it for up to three weeks. Under normal circumstances, it will be clear and the gravity down to zero (1.000) in about ten days. Don't worry about the extra time involved in making beer this way, inasmuch as your beer is aging in the carboy and will be ready that much sooner after bottling. In any case, when these two things occur, i.e., the brew is reasonably clear and the gravity is down to 1.000, the time has come for bottling.

Now take those two cups of sugar saved from your 4 lb. Siphon off about two pints of beer into a clean saucepan, warm on the stove, and dissolve the two cups of sugar to make a beer sugar syrup. Be sure the saucepan is big enough, because the mixture will foam all over the stove if it's not, and annoy your wife somewhat. When this is ready, siphon off the rest of the beer into your clean primary fermenter, being careful not to disturb the yeast sediment.

Save your yeast. At this time you can get your yeast back for your next brew by swirling the sediment in the bottom of the carboy and, using a small funnel, pour it into a clean beer bottle and cap immediately. Place this bottle in the crisper part of your refrigerator where it won't freeze. The next time you make beer you will not have to grow your yeast but merely take this bottle from the refrigerator open it and add it to the "wort" when the wort is properly cooled. This yeast starter will be good in the refrigerator for approximately three to five weeks in the case of Lager yeast and two to three weeks for Ale yeast.

Now that we have the clear beer in the primary fermenter and the gravity is 1.000, stir in the syrup, making sure it is thoroughly distributed, but do not aerate the beer too much. At the same time you can be stirring in the teaspoonful of Heading Liquid. The gravity of this mixture should be approximately 1.005. We will assume that you have already prepared your five dozen bottles, that they are thoroughly clean and standing in a convenient place to be filled to within one inch of the cap. It does not matter if they are wet inside, in fact, it may make it easier to fill them by reducing the foaming. Cap them immediately and place in a temperature of 60°–70° F. for ten days and then chill and try the results of your labour.

For Ale use the same recipe with the addition of 1 oz. of Gypsum, and Ale instead of Lager beer yeast.

The critical factors in producing Lager is that a low fermenting temperature should exist from beginning to finish. Primary fermentation should be in either plastic or crockery, well guarded from the air, and should at no time involve a temperature above 65° F., and preferably not above 60. Before it has completely worked out, it is important to move the lager into a carboy and attach a fermentation lock, not gallon jugs but glass or plastic carboys. It should be Lagered at a temperature of around 45°–50° F., or lower, for at least one month, then carefully siphoned off the lees and 12 oz. of corn sugar added to five gallons, plus a teaspoon of heading liquid and a teaspoon of ascorbic acid. Then of course it is essential, as all Canadian beer is normally bottled and crown capped, that the same procedure be followed here. It should stand in the bottle for at least three weeks to a month and is not likely to be at its peak much before three months from the outset of fermentation.

Ingredients:

2 tins (2½ lb. each) light malt extract
2 oz. of Brewer's gold or cluster hops
¼ oz. Kent Finishing hops
4 lb. corn sugar
5 Imperial gallons of water
2 teaspoons of salt
1 teaspoon of citric acid
1 teaspoon of Grey Owl yeast energiser
1 teaspoon of heading liquid
½ teaspoon of Clarospane beer finings
½ teaspoon of grape tannin
Grey Owl lager beer yeast (dry or liquid)
Starting gravity: 43 to 45
Terminal gravity: 1.003
The method is the same as for Canadian Light Lager.

DRIED MALT EXTRACT

The dried powder malt extract now on the market is rather pleasanter to handle than the sticky, liquid variety, although a little more expensive.

In each of these German recipes, boil the dried malt and hops in the water for half an hour. Strain into fermentation jar or jars to take two gallons, cool to 70° F., add yeast and nutrient, fit air lock and leave to ferment in warm room for seven to eight days. "Prime" as directed under that heading, and bottle.

Light Lager: 2½ lb. dried malt extract, 2 oz. hops, 2 gallons of water, beer yeast.

Lager (Pilsener style): 4½ lb. dried malt extract, 1 oz. hops, 2 gallons water, beer yeast.

Lager: (Munich style): 5 lb. dried malt extract, ½ oz. of caramel, 1 oz. hops, 4 gallons water, beer yeast.

Dark Beer or Porter: 6½ lb. dried malt extract, 1 oz. of caramel, 3 gallons water, beer yeast.

Ale: 6½ lb. dried malt extract, 3 gallons water, 2 oz. hops, beer yeast.

Mock Beers

TRUE beer, of course, is that made from malt and hops, but there are many other "beers", many of them delightful drinks in their own right, and some of them of undoubted therapeutic value. It is fun to experiment with them, and to produce unusual drinks which can NOT be purchased at the local.

APPLE ALE
(Cider)

Ingredients:

3 lb. apples (windfalls will do)	½ teaspoon cinnamon
1 oz. root ginger	1½ lb. white sugar
½ teaspoon cloves	1 gallon water
	Yeast and nutrient

Method:

Wash the apples, cutting out any damaged portions, and grate or mince. Add the water, cold, and the yeast and nutrient, cover with a thick cloth, and leave in a warm room for a week, stirring thoroughly daily. Strain on to the sugar, bruised ginger, cloves and cinnamon, and press out as much extra juice from the pulp as possible by squeezing it in a cloth. Stir vigorously, cover, and leave for about five days. Strain into screw-stoppered flagons. Store in a cool place and the ale will be ready to drink after about another fortnight.

★
BEETROOT BEER

Ingredients:

1 lb. beetroot	1 gallon water
½ lb. malt extract	Yeast
½ lb. brown sugar	

Method:

Wash and slice the beetroot and bring to the boil in the water; simmer for ten minutes. Strain on to the malt extract and sugar, stir well to dissolve, cool to 70° F., then add yeast. Ferment for three days, then siphon into screw-stopper flagons, having first funnelled the level teaspoon of sugar into each. Stand in a cool place for ten days before drinking.

★

BRAHN ALE!

Ingredients:

1 lb. bran	Gravy browning
2 oz. dried hops	Yeast and nutrient
2 lb. Demerara sugar	3 gallons water

Method:

Put two gallons of water in a 3-gallon boiler, and put third gallon by. Bring to boil. Add sugar, 2 ozs. dried hops (buy Heath and Heather packeted hops from chemists), bran, and 2 teaspoonsful of gravy browning (the liquid variety—which is only caramel colouring). Boil gently for 1½ hours. Strain through muslin into crock and on to third gallon of cold water. Leave to cool until blood heat, then pour into three 1-gallon jars, filling to shoulder only. Add brewer's yeast, if obtainable, or dried yeast, fit traps and leave for seven days (in room temperature of 65°). Then siphon into ½-gallon bottles (or smaller ones if these are not available) cork really tightly, tie down corks. The beer may be drunk after another week, but will not be really clear. To clarify, it should be kept at least three weeks after bottling in a cool place. And keep an eye on those corks! This is an excellent and really cheap ale, and may be made week by week to accumulate a quantity, each fresh brew being put on to part of the lees of the former one, and the surplus yeast thrown away or used for other purposes. If this system is to be followed it pays to obtain a small quantity of true brewer's yeast initially, and it can then be kept going for several months. This bran ale costs about 5p a gallon.

CHERRY ALE

Ingredients:

2 pints Morello cherries	2 quarts water
4 lb. sugar	Yeast and nutrient
2 quarts brown ale	

Method:

Prick or bruise the cherries and pour over them the boiling water. Add the sugar and stir well to dissolve. Then add the brown ale. Cool to 70° F. before adding the yeast and nutrient. Ferment "on the pulp" for a week, then strain into a fermenting jar and ferment in a warm room until specific gravity drops to 1010, then siphon into screw-stoppered flagons into each of which a level teaspoon of castor sugar has been funnelled. Store for several months before drinking.

★
CIDER
(Apple Beer)

Any apples will do, windfall or otherwise, but cider apples or cooking apples are best. Wash them, and then chop them into small pieces with a chopping knife, or crush them with an apple-crusher, or with a piece of heavy timber in a half-tub. Press out the juice with a press or by means of a juice extractor and fill your fermenting vessel. Keep a little spare juice in a separate covered jug for "topping up". After a few days, if kept in a warm place, the juice will start fermenting. The container should be stood on a tray because for a while froth will pour out of the neck of the jar. Wipe this off and keep the jar topped up with the surplus juice. When the ferment quietens wipe the jar and tray clean and fit a fermentation trap. When fermentation has ceased bottle in screw-stopper flagons or strong bottles.

★
DANDELION BEER

Ingredients:

½ lb. young dandelion plants	1 gallon water
1 lb. Demerara sugar	½ oz. root ginger
1 lemon	1 oz. cream of tartar
Yeast	

Method:

This is a pleasant drink and is said to be good for stomach disorders. The young plants should be lifted in the spring, and well washed. Leave the thick tap roots but remove the fibrous ones. Put the plants, the well bruised ginger and the rind of the lemon (excluding any white pith) in the water and boil for 20 minutes. Strain on to the sugar, the juice of the lemon and cream of tartar, and stir until all is dissolved. Cool to 70° F., add yeast, and ferment (covered) in a warm place for three days. Bottle in screw-stopper bottles.

★ ELDERFLOWER BEER

Ingredients:

1 pint elderflowers (not pressed down)	1 lemon
	1 lb. sugar
1 gallon water	Yeast and nutrient

Method:

Squeeze out the lemon juice and put into a bowl with the elder florets and sugar, then pour over them the boiling water. Infuse for 24 hours, closely covered, then add yeast. Ferment for a week in a warm room, then strain into screw-stopper flagons. Store in a cool place for a week, after which the beer will be ready for drinking.

★ GINGER BEER

Ingredients:

1 oz. root ginger	1 lemon
½ oz. cream of tartar	1 gallon water
1 lb. white sugar	Yeast and nutrient

Method:

The ginger should be crushed and then placed in a bowl with the sugar, cream of tartar and lemon peel (no white pith). Bring the water to the boil and pour it over the ingredients. Stir well to dissolve the sugar, then allow to cool to 70° F. before adding the lemon juice, yeast and nutrient. Cover closely and leave in a warm room for 48 hours, then stir, strain into screw-stopper flagons and store in a cool place. The beer is ready to drink in three to four days.

★ HONEY BOTCHARD

Ingredients:

1 oz. hops	1 gallon water
1¼ lb. honey	Yeast and nutrient

Method:

Bring the water to the boil, add the hops and honey, and simmer for 30 minutes. Strain the liquid, allow to cool to

70° F., and add yeast and nutrient. Ferment in a warm room for ten days, then siphon into screw-stopper flagons. Store in a cool place for at least a month.

★
HOW TO START A GINGER BEER PLANT

Grow a Ginger Beer Plant with 2 oz. baker's yeast (buy it at a baker's where bread is baked on the premises). Put the yeast into a jar and add ½ pint water, 2 level teaspoons of sugar, and 2 level teaspoons of ground ginger.

Feed it each day for the next seven to ten days. Add 1 teaspoon of sugar and 1 teaspoon of ground ginger. You will see your "plant" growing day by day.

Strain it. Now strain the mixture through a piece of muslin or a very fine household sieve (keep the sediment) and add to the liquid the juice of 2 lemons, 1 lb. granulated sugar and 1 pint boiling water. Stir until the sugar has dissolved, then make up to one gallon with cold water.

Bottle it. Put the ginger pop into bottles, filling to about three inches from the top, and leave for two hours, taking care not to put them on a stone floor, unless standing on a piece of wood. Then cork lightly. Keep for seven to ten days before drinking.

And start again. The sediment you had left when you strained the mixture is divided into two and put into separate glass jars. And you're back in the brewing business again! But now you have two plants instead of one. If one plant is enough for you, give the other to a friend and give him the recipe. To your sediment add half a pint of cold water and carry on as before from "Feed it . . ."

★
HOP BEER (1)

Ingredients:

5 oz. hops	2 level teaspoonfuls
8 gallons water	granulated yeast and
3 lb. brown sugar	nutrient

Method:

Boil the hops and water together slowly for about 40–50 minutes, strain over the sugar, and allow to cool. When tepid add the yeast. Turn into a pan or tub to ferment for four days (at 65° F., up to a week if temperature is lower), then bottle.

101

Tie down corks. Can be drunk within a fortnight but may take a month really to clear.

HOP BEER (2)

Ingredients:

½ oz. hops	1 gallon water
1 lb. white sugar	½ oz. root ginger (crushed)
½ teaspoonful caramel	Yeast and nutrient

Method:

Boil all the ingredients except yeast in the water for an hour, and then make up to one gallon if necessary. Strain, cool to 70° F., and add yeast and nutrient. Leave 48 hours in a warm place, closely covered, then siphon off (without disturbing yeast deposit) into screw-stopper flagons, standing them in a cool place. Ready to drink in a week.

HOREHOUND BEER

Ingredients:

4 oz. horehound	1 gallon water
4 oz. gentian root	½ oz. capsicums
1 lemon	2 oz. calumba root
¾ lb. Demerara sugar	Yeast and nutrient

Method:

This recipe from a Lancashire brewing friend, makes, he says, an excellent tonic beer. Put the horehound, bruised capsicums, gentian, calmus root and lemon peel (omitting any white pith) into a polythene bucket and pour over them the water, boiling. Cover and leave for 12 hours. Put the sugar into a boiler, strain the liquid on to it, and heat and stir until all sugar is well and truly dissolved. Cool to 70° F., transfer to fermenting jar, and add yeast and nutrient. Ferment in warm room for three days, then siphon carefully into quart screw-stopper flagons. Store in cool place for a week before drinking.

NETTLE BEER

Ingredients:

2 gallons young nettles	2 oz. hops
¼ oz. root ginger	4 oz. sarsaparilla
4 lb. malt	2 gallons water
1 level teaspoonsful	1½ lb. sugar
granulated yeast	2 lemons

Method:

Choose young nettle tops. Wash and put into a saucepan with water, ginger, malt, hops and sarsaparilla. Bring to the boil and boil for a quarter of an hour. Put sugar into a large crock or bread pan and strain the liquor on to it; add the juice of the two lemons. Stir until the sugar has dissolved, and allow to cool to 70° F., keeping pan covered, then stir in the yeast. Keep the crock (covered) in a warm room for three days, then strain the beer into bottles, cork, and tie down or wire the corks. Keep the beer in a cool place for a week before drinking—and keep an eye on the corks! This makes an excellent summer drink and should be made in May.

★
PARSNIP STOUT

Ingredients:

3½ lb. parsnips	1 tablespoon caramel gravy
1 gallon water	browning *or* ¼ lb. black
1 oz. hops	malt
½ lb. malt extract	1¼ lb. Demerara sugar
Yeast	

Method:

Scrub the parsnips, slice them in ½-in. slices. Bring the water to the boil, add the parsnips, hops, and caramel colouring (or black malt) and boil for 20 minutes, then strain on to the malt extract and sugar. Stir well to dissolve. Cool to 70° F., then add yeast and nutrient, cover well, and leave in a warm place for seven days. Then siphon into screw-stopper flagons and store in a cool larder for a fortnight before drinking.

★
SPRUCE BEER

To make the beer the recipe is as follows:

Melt 2 lb. sugar, treacle, essence of malt, molasses, or honey, into a gallon of hot water, put in cask or fermentation vessel, add one gallon cold water and 2 tablespoonfuls of the essence of spruce. Spruce essence can be purchased from winemaking supplies firms and from some branches of principal chain chemists. When the must is tepid add ale yeast. Ferment for two days and bottle. It will be ready for use within one week.

TREACLE ALE

Ingredients:

½ lb. Golden Syrup	1 oz. hops
½ lb. black treacle	1 gallon water
½ lb. Demerara sugar	Yeast and nutrient

Method:

Bring the water to the boil, add the hops, syrup, treacle and sugar, and simmer for 45 minutes. Strain, cool to 70° F., add yeast and nutrient, and ferment for at least a week before bottling in screw-stopper flagons.

★
COCK ALE

In a 100-year-old book on brewing we came across the following recipe for a fearsome brew, "Cock Ale":

"Take 10 gallons of ale and a large cock, the older the better; parboil the cock, flay him, and stamp him in a stone mortar until his bones are broken (you must draw and gut him when you flay him), then put the cock into two quarts of sack, and put to it five pounds of raisins of the sun, stoned; some blades of mace, and a few cloves; put all these into a canvas bag, and a little before you find the ale has been working, put the bag and ale together into a vessel. In a week or nine days bottle it up; fill the bottle but just above the neck, and give it the same time to ripen as other ale."

Rather amusedly, and entirely by way of experiment, it was decided to try this, on a one-gallon quantity. Astonishingly, it made an excellent ale, nourishing and strong-flavoured, of the "barley wine" type; well worth trying.

All you need are some pieces of cooked chicken, and a few chicken bones, all well crushed or minced (about a tenth of the eatable portion of the bird), half a pound of raisins, a very little mace, and one (or, if you like, two) cloves. Soak these for 24 hours in half a bottle of your strongest white country wine.

Then make one gallon of beer as described in our malt extract section (p. 82 et seq.), using 1 lb. malt extract, 1 oz. hops, ½ lb. Demerara sugar, 1 gallon water, yeast and nutrient. Add the whole of your cock mixture to the fermenting must, to the fermenting wort at the end of the second day. Fermentation will last six or seven days longer than usual and the ale should be matured at least a month in bottle.

Serving your beers

SERVING YOUR BEERS

THE rule is: drink when clear, serve cool. There is bound be some sediment, which will cloud the drink if carelessly poured. Take a quart jug and have it by your hand, or set out your two pint tankards or four smaller glasses so that you can pour continuously without having to return the bottle to the vertical. Unscrew the bottle's stopper—with caution; you may have over-primed the bottle.

Hold the jug or other receptacle at a slant in one hand and gently tilt the bottle in the other, so that the beer slides out slowly against the side of it.

Avoid the uneven flow that comes of pouring too fast; it will stir up the sediment. Watch the colour of the beer as you pour and stop the flow smartly as soon as you see it becoming cloudy. You will be left with a couple of inches of yeasty beer in the bottom of the bottle. Drink it down yourself and know what good health is, or pour it into a spare flagon, as already suggested, with other dregs to settle. If you bungle the pouring and the drink is cloudy don't apologise. You are only giving others a share in the most nourishing part of the brew, instead of keeping it for yourself!

"LIVELY" BEER

Sometimes in spring or summer, usually at the onset of a warm spell, you will get an extra vigorous fermentation in the flagon, so that the beer is over-"lively". When you unscrew the stopper there may even be a "pheep!" instead

SERVING YOUR BEER

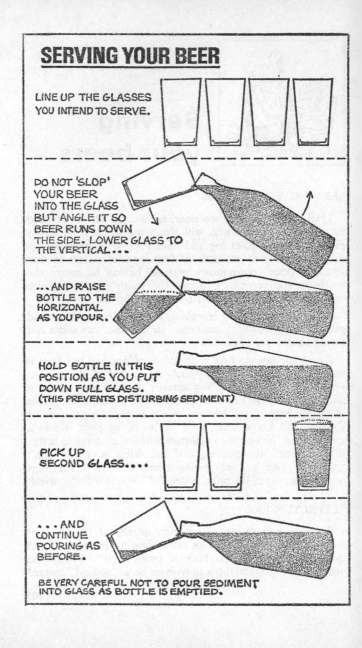

LINE UP THE GLASSES YOU INTEND TO SERVE.

DO NOT 'SLOP' YOUR BEER INTO THE GLASS BUT ANGLE IT SO BEER RUNS DOWN THE SIDE. LOWER GLASS TO THE VERTICAL . . .

. . . AND RAISE BOTTLE TO THE HORIZONTAL AS YOU POUR.

HOLD BOTTLE IN THIS POSITION AS YOU PUT DOWN FULL GLASS. (THIS PREVENTS DISTURBING SEDIMENT)

PICK UP SECOND GLASS . . . .

. . . AND CONTINUE POURING AS BEFORE.

BE VERY CAREFUL NOT TO POUR SEDIMENT INTO GLASS AS BOTTLE IS EMPTIED.

of a gentle hiss and the beer will foam out vigorously. At times it will send up a spout of foaming beer like a fountain, to the detriment of the ceiling and paintwork! And (what is perhaps even worse, in a beer drinker's opinion) all the yeast sediment will rise so much as to make the beer horribly cloudy and undrinkable.

There is only one solution. Wipe all the bottles clean and stand them in the sink. Then release the stoppers and let the bottles foam naturally. Let the process continue until no more froth issues from the bottles (although there may still be a head inside them) then screw down once more, wipe the bottles clean, and store for 48 hours, by which time the beer will be clear again, and drinkable, its liveliness normal.

Not much beer will be lost, except in severe cases, for usually only foam issues, but even this can be saved and poured back into the bottles if you stand the flagons in a clean bowl (not one which has held detergent) or half cask and collect the overflow.

Another way is to insert a cork and length of tubing into each bottle and drain off the froth into fresh containers as publicans do with casks which are too lively.

EXHIBITING AND JUDGING

Brewing has now attained the same stature as winemaking as regards competitions, for the Amateur Winemakers National Guild of Judges now includes a most useful chapter on beer judging in its handbook for judges, show organisers, and competitors (*Judging Home Made Wines and Beers*, 25p), which will well repay reading.

The Guild sets out the main types of beer, and their characteristics, and explains what the judge will be looking for—clean, sound bottles; clean stoppers with sound rubber washers, an air space of $\frac{1}{2}$ inch to $\frac{3}{4}$ inch, a firm yeast deposit, if any, a good head and head retention, coupled with a small and lively "head" (the bubbles), a satisfactory aroma, and the correct body and flavour for that particular type of beer. Normally points will be awarded as follows: 2 for bottling, 4 for bouquet, 4 for condition and clarity, and 20 for taste and flavour.

You may care not only to become an exhibitor, but eventually to become a judge as well, for judges are in great demand; again, the handbook will be your guide to success, and you will eventually be able to take the Guild's qualifying examination.

109

INDEX

Other AW Books

FIRST STEPS IN WINEMAKING
> The acknowledged introduction to the subject. Unbeatable at the price.
> **C. J. J. Berry**

SCIENTIFIC WINEMAKING—made easy
> The most advanced and practical textbook on the subject.
> **J. R. Mitchell, L.I.R.C., A.I.F.S.T.**

THE WINEMAKER'S COOKBOOK
> Gives a whole range of dishes using exciting your homemade wine.
> **Tilly Timbrell and Bryan Acton**

WINEMAKING AND BREWING
> The theory and practice of winemaking and brewing in detail.
> **Dr. F. W. Beech and Dr. A. Pollard**

GROWING GRAPES IN BRITAIN
> Indispensable handbook for winemakers whether they have six vines or six thousand.
> **Gillian Pearkes**

"AMATEUR WINEMAKER" RECIPES
> Fascinatingly varied collection of over 200 recipes.
> **C. J. J. Berry**

WINEMAKING WITH CANNED AND DRIED FRUIT
> How to make delightful wines from off the supermarket shelf.
> **C. J. J. Berry**

PRESERVING WINEMAKING INGREDIENTS
> Includes drying, chunk bottling, deep freezing, chemical preservasion, etc.
> **T. Edwin Belt**

130 NEW WINEMAKING RECIPES
>Superb collection of up-to-date recipes.
>C. J. J. Berry

RECIPES FOR PRIZEWINNING WINES
>Produce superb wines for your own satisfaction!
>Bryan Acton

WHYS AND WHEREFORES OF WINEMAKING
>Assists the winemaker to *unuerstand* what he is doing.

COMMONSENSE WINEMAKING
>Practical, no-frills primer in winemaking.
>Anne Parrack

HOW TO MAKE WINES WITH A SPARKLE
>Discover the secrets of producing Champagne-like wine of superb quality.
>J. Restall and D. Hebbs

MAKING WINES LIKE THOSE YOU BUY
>Imitate commercial wines at a fraction of what they would cost to buy.
>Bryan Acton and Peter Duncan

THE GOOD WINES OF EUROPE
>A simple guide to the names, types and qualities of wine.
>Cedric Austin

ADVANCED HOME BREWING
>The most advanced book on home brewing available in this country.
>Ken Shales

HOME BREWING SIMPLIFIED
Detailed recipes for bottled and draught beer plus knowhow.

WOODWORK FOR WINEMAKERS
Make your own wine press, fermentation cupboard, fruit pulper, bottle racks, etc.
C. J. Dart and D. A. Smith

BREWING BETTER BEERS
Explains many finer points of brewing technique.
Ken Shales

HINTS ON HOME BREWING
Concise and basic down to earth instructions on home brewing.
C. J. J. Berry

MAKING MEAD
The only full-length paperback available on this winemaking speciality.
Bryan Acton and Peter Duncan

PLANTS UNSAFE FOR WINEMAKING
—includes native and naturalised plants, shrubs and trees.
T. Edwin Belt

GROWING VINES
Down-to-earth book for the viticulturist.
N. Poulter

PROGRESSIVE WINEMAKING
500 pages, from scientific theory to the production of quality wines at home.
Peter Duncan and Bryan Acton

DURDEN PARK BEER CIRCLE BOOK OF RECIPES
How to make a whole range of superb beers.
Wilf Newsom

WINEMAKER'S DICTIONARY
The most comprehensive and readily available mine of information. Most easily consulted reference book for winemakers, lecturers and shop staffs.
Peter McCall

100 WINEMAKING PROBLEMS ANSWERED
If you have a winemaking problem you are sure to find the answer in this new book by author, wine judge and lecturer, Cedric Austin, who over the years has compiled the most common faults and problems that beset the winemaker and answered them in one handy book.
Cedric Austin

WINEMAKING WITH CONCENTRATES
For the first time we publish a book entirely devoted to making wine with the various fruit juice and concentrates now available to the home winemaker. Either a British or Canadian edition is available. Please state which you require.
Peter Duncan

OFF-DUTY WINEMAKING
This book has been written to allow the newcomer to winemaking to make his or her first gallon of wine with the minimum of fault and subsequent disappointment. Easy to read, easier-to-follow instructions.

THE BIG BOOK OF BREWING
This "fat paperback" is the most advanced textbook for any home brewer covering all aspects of the craft. 256 pp., fully illustrated with photographs and line drawings.
Dave Line

BREW YOUR FAVOURITE PUB BEERS
Do not be restricted to drinking what your local brewery dictates. Now you can, with the help of this book by T. Edwin Belt, brew the beer that was once available over the bar.
T. Edwin Belt

MAKING CIDER
The only book currently available on this fascinating and ultra-British craft. Recipes for sweet, dry, still and sparkling cider. And cider cookery.
Jo Deal

WINES FROM YOUR VINES
The logical sequence to Mr. Poulter's first book 'Growing Vines'. Readable and very practical, covering all aspect of winemaking from grapes.
N. Poulter

WILD PLANTS FOR WINEMAKING
The Countrymans' or womans' guide to picking programmes throughout the seasons. With easy reference, plants are under the heading of the month they appear in fruit or flower. Ideal for town-dwelling maker of country wines. 87 pp.
T. Edwin Belt

EXPRESS WINEMAKING
Select your own ingredients, make good sound wines, yet have them ready for drinking in a month (or ess).
Ren Bellis

The book for all who want to mash TRUE BEERS of quality

THE BIG BOOK OF BREWING

by Dave Line

The well-known 'AW' contributor

FULL INSTRUCTIONS ON HOW TO MASH AND CONTROL QUALITY WITH EASE

---

only **£1.50** postage 35p

Available from
**Amateur Winemaker Publications Ltd.
South St., Andover, Hants**